The Challenge of Leadership

Is there an intimate relationship between liberal arts and management?

Are liberal arts programs for executives a passing fad, or a pioneer movement in fundamental executive education?

How can a knowledge of the liberal arts add to a manager's understanding of his ideal role?

These are just some of the questions dealt with in this provocative discussion of the growing relationship between liberal education and the successful practice of management.

Top men in the fields of industry and education analyze the type of leadership that is needed to handle the complex affairs of a business community. And they assess the contribution that humanistic studies and programs (such as the Bell Telephone and Aspen programs) are making to the development of creative, self-reliant executives who can meet the business and social responsibilities of the Atomic Age.

Toward the Liberally Educated Executive—a timely book on a vital problem . . . complete with the names and addresses of institutes which sponsor liberal education programs for executives and samples of the booklists used in such courses.

Other MENTOR Books You Will Enjoy

Toward the Liberally Educated Executive

Edited by Robert A. Goldwin
Charles A. Nelson

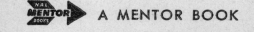 A MENTOR BOOK

Published by THE NEW AMERICAN LIBRARY

Introduction

During the last seven years a good deal of discussion has taken place about the role of liberal education in the development of executive talent for business. This discussion, some of it highly argumentative, has already provoked action designed to demonstrate in practice what liberal education for executives really is and what it has to contribute to executive development. Programs, variously organized, are currently being offered by the University of Pennsylvania, Wabash College, Southwestern at Memphis, Pomona College, the University of Denver, the University of Akron, Northwestern University, the Aspen Institute, and the American Foundation for Continuing Education. Much of the stimulus to businessmen to consider the merits of liberal education has come from the Humanities Center for Liberal Education and its imaginative director, Dr. Max H. Goldberg.

This little book is designed to illustrate three propositions which are fundamental to an understanding of the education of executives in our time.

The first is that the tasks executives have begun to face today and will inescapably confront tomorrow, arising out of the economic and social roles of corporations in American life, are of a magnitude that cannot even be properly grasped, let alone successfully dealt with, except by men with "big" minds.

Second, that in terms of education, the best way to cultivate the requisite "bigness" of mind is through the liberal studies, conceived as those areas of knowledge which enlarge the understanding and deepen the insights of men with regard both to men themselves and men in their social relationships, and which, at their highest levels, assist them to develop the capacity successfully to deal with these abstract ideas that illuminate and allow them more wisely to control the world in which they live.

And, finally, that since the needs of men for understanding and insight are never wholly met—that no man can ever congratulate himself that he has all the understanding and insight he needs—he should early in life acquire the habit of turning to the liberal studies in his leisure that he may refresh himself and go on growing. Liberal education, in short, should be continuous throughout life.

It is not assumed in these pieces that executive development can be wholly based on liberal education. There is unquestionably a body of knowledge all executives must have. It consists of two parts: general vocational knowledge properly to be acquired in schools, specific vocational knowledge properly to be acquired "on the job." But it is here argued that the liberal studies add a dimension to executive training without which executives will be unable to measure up to the challenges they confront and will continue to confront in the foreseeable future.

Approaching this point the other way around, it must not be forgotten that liberal education is a vastly important "thing in itself"—that it embodies a cluster of values of high significance in themselves and for themselves, quite apart from their specific utility to men pursuing a particular vocation. This, too, is recognized in these selections; and the argument pursued is that executives need to appropriate values from liberal education without getting the idea that they are either going over to it as the whole of their training, or wholly taking it over as an adjunct to their vocational development.

Full justice cannot be done to these complex matters in a slim volume like this one. No pretension is made that the full range of the discussion of the role of the liberal studies in executive training has been illustrated here. The purpose of this book is to inform readers that there is a growing movement in the direction of liberal education for executives and to allow some of the chief spokesmen of this movement to present their supporting arguments. We hope thus to arouse interest in the subject and to encourage the development of more adult liberal education programs for management.

C. Scott Fletcher

C. SCOTT FLETCHER, *President*
The Fund for Adult Education

White Plains, New York
July, 1960

Contents

gilbert w. chapman

Specific Needs for Leadership in Management*

NOT SINCE THE EARLIEST COMMUNICATION OF KNOWLEDGE HAS education been so much a subject of public discussion as it is today. Many people far removed from the academic world have become interested in this subject. This has occurred as the result of a widespread realization that our educational capabilities have not kept pace with many of our national needs.

It is a healthy sign that more and more public officials, business executives and trade-union leaders are acutely aware that general problems of education belong not to a small segment of society, but to all of us. The educators want it that way. The responsibility for good education is ours as much as it is theirs. It is a universal problem which bears upon the continued preservation of our free society; its solution will come only from the joint effort of all of us.

Foremost among the groups looking for an answer to the problem is American industry. In these times of revolutionary scientific developments, industry is under a constant, pressing need for scientists and engineers capable of maintaining, directing and advancing our technology. We are also confronted by a growing need for more executive leaders, not only to insure the long-range continuity of management, but also to make certain that today we have men capable of handling the complex affairs of modern corporations.

The future security of this country and the world rests upon the ability of our educational system to develop the highly educated man. Well-balanced maturity, which is essential to our society, must emanate from the universities. We shall need well-trained and analytical minds that can appraise the problems that surround them. In the days ahead, which will be full of international tension and great economic challenge, the moral and spiritual strength which comes with the educated mind will be essential to the preservation of our society. . . .

If our country is to continue to grow and prosper materially and spiritually, there must be a constant exchange of ideas,

* By permission of Gilbert W. Chapman and The Humanities Center for Liberal Education.

needs and ambitions between the educator and the industrialist. This type of co-operation will give rise to a real understanding of each other's problems, and the realization of our common goals. America's role of leadership in world affairs rests upon our political stability, educational growth and industrial democracy. Whether the entire non-Communist world will live or die depends upon the success or failure of American capitalism. What we do or fail to do has a world significance. American corporation executives carry a large share of the burden of this responsibility. These men, depending upon the size and nature of the companies which employ them, make decisions, project plans and weigh problems which in their effects reach quite beyond immediate corporate goals with significant reflection in world affairs. A simple illustration of this is the content and character of overseas promotion and advertising sponsored by American companies. Our own government now recognizes that how we advertise and what we advertise abroad may either advance or retard our foreign policy. American industry has invested large sums in plants abroad and we employ great numbers of citizens of other countries. We buy and sell goods and services all over the globe and we function as the nuclear center of the entire free world.

To meet the challenge of industry's new responsibility in the world requires a cultivation of mind and outlook that must come from the educational institutions of our land. My undergraduate days were spent in a school of engineering. After four years of this highly specialized training, I immediately began my business career in an American corporation. Since that time, it has become increasingly apparent to me that the problems of an executive become less specialized and more general or basic as the man advances toward the top. The specialist cannot function effectively at the top level of management if all he brings to it is his specialty. At that level, the daily problems call for broad general knowledge, open-mindedness, an understanding of human nature, an insight into human frailties, a fairness of mind, a clarity of thought—all these beyond the ordinary knowledge of a complex business problem. There must be an intellectual cultivation through which an individual views the main current of the life around him.

The specialist is not excluded from a career in top management; it would be a little ridiculous for an engineer to suggest that. My contention is that the specialty alone, which thrives so well in the laboratory or research center, is in itself not sufficient qualification for top executive responsibility. Let the specialist extend his knowledge into the broader fields of general learning; then he, too, can move ahead—perhaps even more rapidly than others.

The qualifications needed for leadership in industry are developed largely through a liberal arts education. Let us stop for a moment and repeat what is perhaps obvious. The phrase "the liberal arts" means the arts appropriate to a free man. These arts originally were seven: grammar, rhetoric, logic, music, arithmetic, geometry and astronomy. The purpose of these studies was not to fill the human mind with facts; it was to train the student to use his mind, to have intellectual curiosity, taste, moral strength and imagination. The scope of liberal arts has been broadened to include many other disciplines, among them literature, languages and fine arts. For most students, none of these has a specific vocational value, but all of them contribute to the enrichment of intellect and judgment. This enrichment is not produced by superspecialized training. Here the mind is too often isolated and cannot cope with the strangeness of the great outside world, with its social and economic differences, its changing language and shifting customs. We need people who can understand the responsibility of American industry and the influences which radiate from it. This kind of leadership requires a sympathetic knowledge of the people of other countries as well as our own, familiarity with the history of all peoples, their modes and customs. The preparation of this type of leadership must begin in education.

Education must also prepare future industrial leaders for the complexities they will encounter in this vitally expanding American economy. The executive of today and the future will have to make, or participate in the making of, decisions involving an almost limitless number of considerations. He will have to think clearly and systematically, using all the available information to its fullest extent. The corporation can teach the trainee the facts of credit and finance, but there just aren't the time or the facilities to teach him to attack problems logically. If colleges and universities will give courses in general economics to all undergraduates who aspire to careers in industry, so much to the good. But it is more important for educators to train minds to think in an organized fashion. Many young people coming out of college cannot understand the simplest accounting terms. Again, we do not necessarily need courses in reading balance sheets, but certainly we do need some form of intellectual training that will make it possible for the normally intelligent person to understand a balance sheet or, for that matter, anything else he reads.

That brings me to the next problem: the ability to write is as important as the ability to read. Management is deeply involved in the art of communication and often success and profit depend upon it. Eventually, all decisions must be communicated, either orally or in writing. The ability to express oneself and the ability to understand what is expressed are absolute prerequisites for successful executive performance. At the very top, the man who cannot express himself will not be successful; for it is he who must communicate the essential meaning of business decisions and policies to all levels. . . . Without the ability to read intelligently and write coherently, the young man is not a prospect for executive responsibility. A career in industrial leadership offers no prospect of reward to him.

Much of this need can be satisfied by exposing more students, whatever forms of disciplines they are pursuing, to the great literature of our language. I am appalled by the glaring unfamiliarity some young people have with good books. Yet there is no surer way to a good command of English than by reading books. The other values which one derives from books join with the love of music and the arts in the development of a good mind and a good spirit. The humanistic influence of great art is one of the most positive forces in the development of a well-balanced mind, capable of attitudes and beliefs, which can assume responsibility in a free society. The arts bring to a man a sense of peace with the world and a warmth of heart and a love of beauty that will aid in molding that man into a person capable of making great decisions.

Corporate responsibilities are most often met and carried out in group relationships. We hear today frequent reference to the management team. This is a reality. No one man is capable of determining the facts and making all the decisions in the complex industrial economy in which we live and work. To live with one's peers, to have their respect and to have the ability to abide by the decisions of the recognized authority, these are the qualities essential to success. The warmth of feeling and the proper humility which must always underlie relationships with a group are enriched by and perhaps derived from exposure to the humanities at the formative age.

The levels of management must be manned by people who understand others. This is the key to leadership. A corporation is nothing more than a group of men and women, with all the qualities that make the human being so complex. How well the executive understands human nature, inside and outside his own company, will be the ultimate measure of his capacity for leadership. He will learn nothing about this in the laboratory; he will find no blueprint of it on the drawing board. His understanding can only come from living and learning, that is, from experience.

Education, and only education, can start the process to bring this understanding to a person. Some of it perhaps will come from the study of psychology; some of it from the inspiration of great artists and writers; some of it from a study of history, which can so well arouse a deep feeling of respect and humility. The sciences will bring to the young man a discipline of mind, a respect for the truth, a desire for the facts that will stand him in good stead throughout his business career.

Now this may seem to conflict with the currently expressed fear that we have a dearth of scientists and engineers, while the Russians are apparently graduating a tremendous number each year. Let me say directly that I am not recommending the curtailment of specialized training in favor of the liberal arts. I am advocating, in the first place, more general education for our specialists; in the second place, a new, strong emphasis on the liberal arts as a preparation for careers in executive management. Our focus has been sharply drawn to technical training by what seems to be an unsatisfied need for applied scientists and engineers. There should be an equally sharp focus directed to general education so that young men and women will be encouraged to know that this, too, is a road to achievement in industry, and any other field of endeavor. . . .

The need in industry, when boiled down, is simply for men with a well-balanced education. Many institutions of learning realize this need and have revised their curricula so that preparation for engineering and scientific degrees now includes some liberal arts courses. The task ahead is to get other colleges and universities to follow suit. This is made difficult not only by the constant clamor for more specialists but by the fact that many educators feel that the kind of education about which we are talking makes a fuller and happier personal life but has little practical value for the world at large. Actually, however, the men who go through the process of higher education and learn how to lead full and happy lives are exactly the ones best qualified as leaders to carry on the responsibilities of the Atomic Age. What the world needs, and what American business needs, is a steady stream of creative men with a broad knowledge and a capacity for independent thinking. We need men who pursue ideas, who will seek to solve problems, although they may have nothing to do with the immediate business problems before them; men whose thought processes do not end with the business day, who, through their education, have learned that one of the greatest joys in life is to be able to think for oneself.

In calling for greater emphasis on the liberal arts, we are seeking to keep our civilization intact. If its growth is retarded at all, it will be in its spiritual and intellectual fiber. It is here that we need strength if we are to evolve into a happier and more cultured society.

If this philosophy becomes the backbone of our educational system, the highly trained specialist and the liberal-arts student will both benefit by it.

One day, when the social sciences have reached further maturity, we will, perhaps, know more about the sources of human happiness. We do know that these blessings lie deep in the individual: our capacities to think and react to thought, to live by spiritual values, to have understanding and tolerance, to comprehend ideas, to be inspired by greatness and to have a sense of God's presence. Unless our education is directed to the enrichment of these resources, it will fail us in providing our leaders and fail us in our time of danger.

The attention being given to the problem shows that there is a mounting determination to solve it. This flows from our deep-seated belief that the fate of America, the capitalistic system, and the happiness of our people are tied to the future of education. Let it be strong and rich and great in its capacities. Then we will have nothing to fear from any quarter.

francis h. horn

A Lifetime of Learning *

SENATOR FULBRIGHT COMPLAINED THAT ENGINEERS AND BUSINESSMEN, doctors and lawyers, "do not talk up and down and across the whole range of human experience, stimulating and stimulated by that experience, to perfect the spirit of their age in the light of the spirit of all ages. . . ."

We do wrong to suggest that any educational system can in four, or ten times four, years produce the kind of person Mr. Fulbright wants. It is the acceptance, however, of this sanguine view of liberal education that lies behind the almost pathetic pleas of corporation executives for liberally educated college graduates. Part of the trouble springs from their impatience with the lack of ability of college graduates in the area of written and spoken communications. But their great need is for "potential top-management personnel." What industry wants most desperately today is bright college graduates who will quickly become executive vice-presidents and advance the corporation's position vis-à-vis its competitors. The corpora-

* From "Liberal Education Re-examined," *The Harvard Educational Review* (Vol. XXVI, No. 4, Fall, 1956). By permission of *The Harvard Educational Review.*

tions are looking to the colleges for such paragons of virtue and ability that the colleges are making a huge mistake in not saying to industry that they cannot turn out such graduates. What industry wants is individuals who possess "the imaginative comprehension which comes from understanding the whole condition of man," to quote one prominent industrialist. Or, to quote another, "men who understand the whole sweep of modern economic, political and social life." Where is the individual, within or without the university, who could claim such knowledge? Yet this is the type of graduate which industry expects from the liberal-arts colleges. . . .

It is time for educators and laymen alike to stop speaking about a liberal education's being acquired in a college course of 120 weeks' duration. A truly liberal education is the product of a lifetime of learning, study, reflection. Even then few people attain it. The best the college can do is to lay the foundation for a liberal education, to inculcate the habits of mind, breadth of interest and enlargement of spirit which, when continued and enriched during later years, can result in a true liberal education.

e. digby baltzell

Bell Telephone's Experiment in Education*

ON JUNE 23, 1954, THIRTY-ONE CHILDREN AND THEIR PARENTS were enjoying themselves at a picnic on the lawn in front of an old colonial farmhouse in Media, Pennsylvania, a suburb of Philadelphia. Many of the children were a long way from home: Melinda and Gayleen Woodruff lived in Palo Alto, California; Sally, Sue and Cindy Hoverstock came from Houston, Texas; and Judy and Dick Asel had just driven up from Little Rock, Arkansas. They would all be driving home across America the next day. These children had come to visit their fathers, a carefully chosen group of businessmen from the Bell Telephone System, who were celebrating their completion of a novel experiment at the University of Pennsylvania. These young executives were, perhaps more than they knew, pioneers.

Many leaders in American business have been frankly

* From *Harper's* magazine (March, 1955). By permission of Dr. E. Digby Baltzell.

worried about the supply of broadly educated executives for top management positions. Talented and conscientious young men who are now climbing the large corporation ladders too often exhibit the "trained incapacity" of the narrow expert, and for understandable reasons: many of them are recruited from business and engineering schools rather than liberal-arts colleges. Moreover, the pressure of their jobs narrows rather than expands their interests in the world about them.

The Bell System, with more than 700,000 employees, is the biggest industrial organization in America. To keep its tremendous daily traffic of calls, installations and services humming requires, of course, a vast army of technically trained specialists. But there is nothing static about this business and at the policy levels executives are continually forced to solve new problems and find fresh answers to old ones. For some time the Bell System's top management has been worried about over-specialization among its younger executives, the very men who are ultimately going to have to be the System's imagination.

W. D. Gillen, president of the Bell Telephone Company of Pennsylvania and a trustee of the University of Pennsylvania, determined several years ago to find some way of broadening the educational background and expanding the point of view of Bell's most promising young men. In 1952, he discussed with the representatives of the University of Pennsylvania a new kind of education for executive leadership; together they decided that in contrast to the usual executive *training* program, young executives needed a really firm grounding in the humanities or liberal arts. A well-trained man knows *how* to answer questions, they reasoned; an educated man knows *what* questions are worth asking. At the policy level, Bell wanted more of the latter.

Mr. Gillen took the plan to several other presidents of Bell companies and got their support. In the spring of 1953, as a consequence, the Institute of Humanistic Studies for Executives, sponsored by Pennsylvania Bell, came into existence on the campus of the University. Classrooms and administrative space were assigned, and Dr. Morse Peckham, an associate professor of English who had outlined a liberal-arts course for businessmen the previous autumn, took on the job of director.

The first group of Bell executives arrived the following September and, as a member of the faculty assigned to keep close tabs on the experiment, I got to know them and their problems well. There were seventeen of them, a carefully chosen lot from various sections of the country. But they were all from the middle levels of management. Eleven were between thirty-five and forty years of age, three were in their early thirties, and one was forty-eight; their average length of service with the Bell System was thirteen years; all were married and all, save one, were fathers; fifteen were college graduates, nine had B.S. degrees and six had B.A.'s.

Each of them was granted a ten months' leave of absence with full salary from his regular job in order to devote his full time to the Institute. The first nine months of the program included 550 hours of lectures, discussions and seminars. The final four weeks of the program were set aside for a reading period during which the men were entirely on their own.

To jar the businessmen-students out of the job atmosphere from which they had come, the courses were deliberately arranged so as to proceed from unfamiliar ideas and material to those closer to their own lives and experiences. In the early months of the program the men received a highly concentrated dose of systematic logic, the study of Oriental history and art, and the reading of such works as the *Bhagavad-Gita, Monkey* and *The Tale of Genji*—a far cry from the American suburban groove and business routine. By December many of the students were depressed; the "Bagdad Geisha," they felt, was a waste of time.

On the other hand, as the end of the program approached, the men were prepared to bring a wide-ranging intellectual experience to bear on problems much closer to home. In the final and most popular course, American Civilization, they spent twelve weeks discussing such problems as: the making of the Constitution; the Haymarket Riot and the industrialization of America; *Sister Carrie* and the revolution in American sex mores; *Main Street* and the disillusionment of the 1920's; and *The Lonely Crowd* and American character structure. The course was organized on the theory that one approached Carol Kennicott's struggles with Main Street from a broader point of view for having known something about Prince Genji in eleventh-century Japan.

The study of James Joyce's *Ulysses* was the most controversial part of the curriculum. It was the director's pet idea, and he fought for it. To him it symbolized the function of a liberal-arts education—to provide a liberating experience and to stimulate the intellect. He believed that an intensive analysis of Bloom's day in Dublin, June 16, 1904, would do just that. (One of the students sent post cards to the other participants on June 16, 1954. On the cards was written: "Happy Bloom's Day.")

The *Ulysses* course consisted of eight three-hour seminars for each of two groups of students. Fortified with the extensive "pony" literature on Joyce, dictionaries of mythology, encyclopedias and Webster, each man prepared one or more reports for his seminar group.

They found it a challenging, and often exasperating, experience. At the close of each report, there was a sigh of relief from the man who had to report, and a wave of congratulations from the rest of the students. "I was proud of Gene! I never got half the stuff he saw in the chapter when I read it." And neither had anyone else, on even a careful first reading.

The final report in one of the *Ulysses* seminars suggests the tone of the whole program. The man who gave it was an accountant and, incidentally, a musician who had earned his way through college during the Depression by playing in dance bands. Patently cool toward the works of Mr. Joyce, he finally volunteered to report on the "Sirens" section, in which Bloom's extreme loneliness is portrayed in a highly complicated and technical musical theme. His report took just forty-two hours to prepare. "You know, this man Joyce has something for everybody if he looks hard enough. I really got interested in that ——— chapter." The report was so thorough that the instructor had it mimeographed for distribution to the whole seminar group and for the use of his future graduate students.

The Institute courses were taught by several members of the faculty from the University, supplemented by two professors from Bryn Mawr and Swarthmore Colleges. In addition, to make sure the students came in contact with the best in the intellectual world, each instructor was asked to invite a series of guest lecturers. One hundred and sixty of America's leading intellectuals—including Lewis Mumford, Clyde Kluckhohn, W. H. Auden, Jacques Lipchitz, Delmore Schwartz, Henry S. Commager, Virgil Thomson, Ludwig Lewisohn, David Riesman, and Eric Goldman—visited West Philadelphia that winter.

The guest lecturers were interested both in the nature of the experiment and in the men who were participating in it. In a clubroom rented in a hotel near the University they had a chance to meet the students for informal discussion at the cocktail hour. "You mean," one of them said to me, "that this idea came from the Bell Telephone people!" Public relations cut both ways in these meetings. The distinguished visitors became acquainted with and, above all, were appreciated by the students.

For ten months the seventeen Bell men were kept busy. In addition to the regular classwork, they read constantly (more than the average graduate student); they went on formally planned trips to art galleries, museums and historical sights in Washington, New York and Philadelphia; a block of seats was reserved for them at the Philadelphia Orchestra concerts; and they visited and studied in some of the distinguished examples of residential and institutional architecture in the city. All of the men seemed determined to make the most of the experience. Not only did they want to justify the costs of the program to the Bell System, but they seemed to want to make up for what they had missed in their formal education. "College wasn't like this, or at least I never found it so," some of them said, and one graduate engineer told me: "It was the degree as a ticket to a job, not an education, that we were after in those Depression days."

In Utopia, perhaps, men will be "trained" in their teens and "educated" in their thirties. While twenty may be the best age for learning mathematics, chemistry or engineering, maybe *Hamlet* and *Faust* are better understood in maturity. To these students, a discussion of pragmatism was naturally related to their own anxieties about permissive education (one father, trained in a teachers' college, disciplined his child without feeling guilty about it for the first time during this period); *Babbitt* or C. Wright Mills's *White Collar* suggested disturbing insights into their own lives; and these men who had lived through the Depression knew what Walt Whitman was giving up when he left a well-paying editorship to devote his life to poetry, even if they could not quite understand his motives.

A real education is an emotional as well as an intellectual experience; and there were both pleasant and unpleasant experiences in this first year's experiment. Few of these students, for example, will ever forget the lecture on Leonardo da Vinci in the art class or the reading of Ezra Pound's *Pisan Cantos*.

One morning in May a student described the slide-illustrated lecture on Leonardo to me over a cup of coffee at Horn & Hardart. When the class was over, so his story went, the lights were turned on and the instructor walked out of the room with tears in his eyes; after several minutes of silence, the students filed out behind him. The eyes of this tall, Lincoln-esque executive, a lieutenant commander, USNR, who had seen the bomb damage at Nagasaki, were somewhat moist that morning as he described the lecture on Leonardo.

The poetry of Ezra Pound is still a controversial artistic fact. Whereas many young graduate students follow fashion, and either like Pound or not as the intellectual climate demands, his *Pisan Cantos* were an unpleasant emotional issue at the Institute. On a Wednesday evening in February, during a heated and somewhat tense discussion of Mr. Pound's poetry with a visiting expert from Harvard, there was very little sympathy for either the guest's admiration for the *Pisan Cantos* or his friendship for Mr. Pound. Driving home after the discussion, one of the students said: "You know, I was so upset reading Pound last Monday night that I took two aspirins before going to bed and then got up at two in the morning to take a sedative before finally getting off to sleep. I could not, for the life of me, understand what the man was trying to say in those *Cantos*."

"This is my one big opportunity," one of the men said to me after he had been in the course for several months, "and I mean to make the most of it." This sense of cramming into a short ten months what might have been for many men several years of education raised several questions. Were these men interested primarily in doing a good job in the Institute because it might mean later promotions in the Bell System for them? Having been exposed to an experience that would presumably change their attitudes toward their jobs and their leisure, was there a chance that they would never again be satisfied with the struggle up the corporate ladder? These were questions that those of us on the faculty asked ourselves, and some of the answers became apparent during the course of the year. Others will remain unanswered for some time.

The Institute of Humanistic Studies for Executives, we were confident, introduced seventeen men of affairs to a new world of ideas, new values, new interests, and to a new type of personality, the intellectual; and the men of affairs changed considerably. They have taken to buying books and building their own libraries; they are collecting classical records; they think about replacing "wall-cover" with art in their homes; and they are more aware of the architectural clichés in American suburbs. One of them said to me:

"When my brother-in-law recently gave his daughter a red Buick convertible for a graduation present, my wife and I thought how a trip abroad would have been a much more lasting gift. A year ago we would have taken the convertible for granted."

As the course was drawing to its close, each of its members was asked to fill out an anonymous questionnaire in which he was to give his opinion of the course and the effect it had on him. A number of revealing, if not surprising, changes in attitude came to light. Reading habits, for one thing, had changed. "I'm taking more advantage of library facilities, reading two newspapers, and reviewing several good news magazines," one man said. Another reported, "I approach newspapers and periodicals with much more curiosity and speculation than before; politics make more sense; the art section in *Time* is not only readable but interesting; I read the book-review section in the *New York Times;* questions concerning McCarthyism are thought through with some real attention to ultimate questions."

But perhaps more revealing comments were made by the men at a dinner in May in a private dining room at the Philadelphia Racquet Club, where Cleo Craig, then president of the

American Telephone and Telegraph Company, was the guest of honor. After the entree, Craig asked each of the men to summarize briefly what he had gotten out of the course. It was evident that the men had primarily learned something about themselves.

"When I first went to work for Bell during the Depression, I spent twelve to fourteen months collecting coin boxes," one of them said. "From that time on, I worked all the time and sacrificed everything to get ahead. Now things are different. I still want to get along in the company but I now realize that I owe something to myself, my family and my community."

A second man said: "This course has given me a new interest in my status and my inheritance, and a mode of determining what they are." Another was "less content with personal values than before," and went on to say that the course had "stimulated a creeping discontent and loss of complacency." Finally, one of them summed up his feelings about the program as follows: "Before this course, I was like a straw floating with the current down the stream. The stream was the Bell Telephone Company. I don't think I will ever be like that straw again."

The men all went back to their jobs in July. Almost six months later, during Christmas week, I talked with seven of them and had long letters from three others. Although the effects of such an educational program as this one cannot be measured with any precision, some interesting effects that it has had on the men are already apparent.

In the first place, it must be remembered that they were chosen because of their demonstrated abilities and strong drives toward success in the Bell System. They are, they report, glad to be "in harness" again, and on the whole they have found the transition back to their jobs much easier than getting used to the program of the Institute. One theme runs through their comments on the effects of the program: they have considerably more confidence in themselves, which, in turn, has "created an even stronger desire for more and broader responsibility in the business."

This self-confidence has resulted, they feel, in a greater ability to make decisions. "I think the chief benefit from the program is a kind of emotional detachment. I don't feel the same personal involvement and emotional insecurity about business problems. This increase in objectivity adds to my confidence in taking the risk of decision. I get more sleep now, too!" To find this confidence born of objectivity is all the more gratifying to us at the Institute because several of us visualized the successful business executive as someone who "flew by the seat of his pants," as the saying goes, and possessed some kind of intuitive "feel" for the right decision. Well aware of the archetypical intellectual's difficulty in arriving at decisions because of a tendency to see all sides of every question, we were afraid that the Institute's program might educate this intuitive feel out of these promising young men. The following comment seems to me a wise refutation of these fears:

"I have been much more efficient in organizing the relevant facts and placing alternative courses of action in sharp focus. Although I now see more angles and am less sure that any particular decision is *the* right one, I am aided in making it by the realization that there is probably no *one* right solution to many problems. I am now much less upset, and more able to learn, by mistakes." Another man says of his new sense of perspective and objectivity: "This may sound contradictory, but I find myself to be much more critical than before and, at the same time, much more tolerant."

This confidence and assurance evidently has not been limited to their life in business. One man in a large Midwestern city, for example, talked about the Institute to a social club composed of professional people interested in the arts and literature. He was extremely gratified both by their response to his talk and because he got along with them so well in informal conversation afterward.

These young men of affairs have not become intellectuals. They are not bringing bookish ideas from the program into their business and community life. Rather, they have developed into sympathetic and informed listeners, or catalysts in drawing out other people's interests. As one writes: "A particularly well-read person in the company who used to interest me very little has become a fast friend of mine and is fostering my continued interest in ideas unwittingly. I of course do most of the listening."

What Americans proudly call know-how has produced many things: great corporations, great bombs and a great many automobiles and refrigerators. In the Institute of Humanistic Studies for Executives, however, Bell's high managers are seeking to remedy a weakness in American democracy which Tocqueville discerned over one hundred years ago. "It would seem as if the rulers of our time," he said, "sought only to use men in order to make things great; I wish they would try a little more to make great men; that they set less value on the work, and more value upon the workman."

From the point of view of the Bell System, it is far too early to assess the value of their experiment. But it is perhaps significant that the wives, at the picnic celebrating the completion of the program, provided a large cake with one candle and this inscription: "With Love and Kisses to 'The Humans,' Class of 1954."

wilfred d. gillen

Why Should a Company Spend Money in This Way?*

LESS THAN FIVE YEARS AGO AN IDEA WAS CONCEIVED THAT HAS developed into one of the most exciting and stimulating experiences that could happen to a businessman or to a business institution. I refer to the experiment which is a new approach to the problem of developing future managers for a corporation, known by the high-sounding title of "The Institute of Humanistic Studies for Executives at the University of Pennsylvania." (That title was selected by a member of the faculty, not by us.) . . .

A question often asked is: "Why should a company spend money in this way? Won't an ambitious young man think of these things and get the same information on his own?" Reflection, I think, will indicate that this approach is not practical. Granted that a few exceptional individuals with perhaps a liberal-arts education might have the time, stamina and ability to do the necessary reading and to take an interest in the cultural life of the community; still this will not meet the objectives. We are not looking for areas of learning, nor are we seeking to turn businessmen into connoisseurs of the arts. Rather, we are giving them a chance to find themselves and their places in society by means of a sabbatical leave; to try out their own ideas through reading and discussion with others; and to study under a guided program designed for their needs —of which they may not even be aware. Clearly, it would be impossible for an individual to do this on his own.

We believe . . . that a man must have lived in the world and must have become more mature before he can absorb and appreciate the value of the humanities and be able to profit from them. This is really an experiment in adult education. A few results, however, are known, and I summarize them:

1. There was tremendous enthusiasm on the part of each year's participants. They tell us they have increased per-

* From "The Institute of Humanistic Studies for Executives," *Liberal Adult Education.* By permission of Wilfred D. Gillen and The Fund for Adult Education.

sonal identity and self-realization. In other words, this means that the men know where they are going and why and they also know why they have chosen the path they have.

2. The changes in the men were apparent to those watching them. They have greater intellectual curiosity and self-confidence and are better able to express their ideas.

3. They tell us it has made them better family men, better citizens in their communities and better individuals.

If this is true, and we have sufficient evidence to believe it is, won't they be better telephone men? . . .

If any justification were needed, and I personally don't think it is, for a business to spend its money and man power on experiments of this nature, I would remind you that most corporations today are spending vast sums in technical research. New multimillion-dollar laboratories have been and are being built throughout our country—all vital and necessary for the growth and progress of our industrial civilization. But I submit to you that regardless of how much progress we make in science and technology, we will need broad-gauged men at the helm of management to harness and effectively use these products for the good of society. Therefore, I answer the question with this question: Don't we have the responsibility of trying to train the next generation to cope with the complex problems of the future?

We believe that this is a major responsibility of corporate management today. We are, as I have stressed, trying to make a constructive contribution to meeting what we think is currently the most important problem facing the corporate future. . . .

morris s. viteles

An Evaluation of the Bell Program at the University of Pennsylvania*

IN 1953, AT THE UNIVERSITY OF PENNSYLVANIA, AN INSTITUTE of Humanistic Studies for Executives was initiated, supported completely by the Bell Telephone System. Men with high potential, selected from the third and higher levels of supervision, were released from their jobs to spend a full academic year

* From *Personnel Psychology: A Journal of Applied Research* (Vol. 12, No. 1, Spring, 1959). By permission of Morris S. Viteles and *Personnel Psychology*.

(approximately ten months) at the University. Courses were grouped into four major fields: history, science, philosophy and the arts. The program started with a tool course in Practical Logic and a short transitional course in Business History. The latter was followed by the History of Economic Thought, World Art, History and Aesthetics of Music, Analytical Reading, World Literature, Social Science, Philosophy of Ethics and the History and Meaning of Science. As these more or less specialized courses neared completion, the various areas of knowledge were integrated and related to the present-day world in courses presented during the final weeks, including a detailed study of James Joyce's book about life in a modern city, *Ulysses;* a course in Modern Architecture and City Planning; a course in American Civilization; and, finally, one in Political Science and International Relations.

Teaching methods included lectures, discussions, seminars and field trips. The latter, which represented an enriched educational experience outside of the classroom, included visits to the United Nations Secretariat, Philadelphia Orchestra concerts, trips to New York, Washington and Philadelphia museums, and attendance at lectures, exhibitions and other cultural activities to be found in and around Philadelphia.

The Institute faculty included scholars from the University of Pennsylvania and nearby colleges. In addition, the program included approximately one hundred guest lecturers who were outstanding in their respective fields.

The reading of many books was a strong and central feature of the program of humanistic studies. These were supplied to the student, and represented the nucleus of a substantial library to which, it was hoped, he would keep adding. This was viewed as a significant step in achieving one objective of the program, viz., "to motivate participants to accept the concept of intellectual activity as a never-ending process to be continued throughout life."

Coincident with the inauguration of the program of humanistic studies, a program for evaluating outcomes was also initiated. The Evaluation Survey was designed with the primary purpose of objectively appraising the immediate results of the educational program in the way of enriching the intellectual background, in modifying the attitudes, interests, values of participants, and in the achievement of similar goals.

The survey has yielded findings which make it possible to answer, at least in part, such questions as: Have anticipated goals been achieved? Are individuals enrolled in the educational program different in certain respects at the end of the program from what they were at the start of the program? Are observed changes a matter of chance or can they be related to participation in the educational program?

Evaluation of immediate outcomes has been based on the administration of a series of tests and questionnaires, including measures of knowledge of subject matter, critical thinking, attitudes and values, temperamental traits, and of participants' opinions concerning objectives of the program and of the extent to which these were achieved. Instruments were selected or developed with reference to the specific goals of the program, as formulated when this program was originally outlined.

Administration of the tests and questionnaires to participants immediately *before* and immediately *after* training, i.e., in September of one year and in June of the following year, constitutes a central feature of the survey plan. An additional and highly significant feature is a similarly spaced administration of the tests and questionnaires to a *Control* group, consisting of individuals who were not exposed to the educational program, referred to in this report as the *Untrained* group.

The *Control* group ($N = 16$) was tested in the academic year 1953–54, concurrently with the examination of the first group of men enrolled in the Institute of Humanistic Studies for Executives, designated as *Group 1* ($N = 17$). Application of tests and questionnaires to *Group 2* ($N = 19$) in 1954–55, and to *Group 3* ($N = 21$) in 1955–56, provided the means of examining the consistency of outcomes from the program, from year to year.

In the case of *Group 1* and the *Control* group, an extensive battery, extending over a period of three days, was administered. A number of tests were eliminated; others—particularly the newly standardized *Graduate Record Area Tests*—were substituted for tests administered to *Group 1*, and the testing time was reduced in the case of *Groups 2* and *3*. However, the large majority of the tests and questionnaires which constitute the basis of this report were administered to all three groups. Furthermore, a second *Control* group, designated as *Control 2*, examined in the fall of 1956 and re-examined in the spring of 1957, provided a base for the interpretation of data yielded by tests administered only to *Groups 2* and *3*.

Scores obtained by program participants, and their responses to questionnaires *before* training, have been compared with similar data yielded by the survey instruments *after* training. In addition, such *before* and *after* scores and questionnaire responses have been compared with those of the *Control* group.

Appropriate statistical techniques have been applied to examine the significance of differences between *before* and *after* scores and between *Untrained* (*Control*) and *Trained* groups. The *p* values cited in the present report were derived from the application of the Wilcoxon Matched Pairs Signed Ranks Test.

The scope and cost of the educational program suggest that a stringent level of confidence be applied in the interpretation of findings derived from the Evaluation Survey. In this connection, it is of interest to note that none of the eight differences between *before* and *after* scores of the *Control* groups, presented in Figures 1–7, is significant at or below the .01 level of confidence, and that only one is below the .05 level. By contrast, of the seventeen *before-after* differences applying to the *Trained* groups, thirteen are below the .01 level of confidence, one is at the .01, and one at the .02–.05 level. Furthermore, the remaining two *p* values apply to results yielded by the Conservatism-Radicalism Opinionaire which, as noted below Figure 7, require special consideration by reason of variations among supposedly equivalent forms of the test.

The application to these and other data of a technique developed by R. A. Fisher to determine the combined significance of differences obtained in the testing of successive groups clearly confirms the view that great significance can be attached to the aggregate of observed differences consistently in the same direction yielded by successive *Trained* groups.

Detailed data concerning survey findings, applying to individual groups, are found in earlier, unpublished reports. In such reports, findings are presented bearing upon certain *specific* objectives which cannot be characterized as having been satisfactorily achieved, e.g., improvement of skill in deductive reasoning. Presented below is a delineation of positive outcomes which have appeared *consistently* throughout the first three years of the educational activity. Included, also, is a sampling of figures and associated notes which illustrate the findings upon which the conclusions from the Evaluation Survey are based.

The broadening of cultural, historical and social perspectives of business executives represents one of the major objectives of the program of humanistic studies. Content and teaching methods were designed:

> . . . to indicate the importance, impact, and use of history, science, philosophy, and arts in the world today, particularly as they influence large groups of people such as employees, customers, and stockholders.

. . . to enable the potential future executive to understand and interpret the social, political, and economic changes, both national and world-wide, which will influence the problems of corporate management to an increasingly greater degree in the future.

Such goals cannot be achieved unless program participants acquire increased familiarity with many facts, a large variety of concepts, and with the role played by important figures in the development of the arts, science, social, cultural and ethical and related movements.

Increase in knowledge cannot, however, be considered an achievement of prime consequence in itself. Certainly, from the viewpoint of a program of humanistic education, it is important for executives to learn that Adam Smith was an economist of the eighteenth century, Goya a Spanish painter of the same period, Dostoevski a Russian novelist of the nineteenth century, and so on. It is important for them to know both the meaning and significance of such concepts as laissez faire, field theory, positivism, surrealism and others drawn from varied fields of human knowledge which are familiar to the "knowledgeable citizen." Nevertheless, such accumulated knowledge represents "the mere façade of education," which helps individuals "to be more successful at quiz tests and crossword puzzles,"[1] unless accompanied by an increased understanding and discernment of what *knowledge can perform.*"

Awareness of this situation has led to emphasis on the *understanding and critical evaluation of issues and problems* in the areas of the social sciences and humanities, in assessing the outcomes of the program of humanistic education. Tests and questionnaires have focused attention upon the development of a critical outlook and of skill in making use of materials covered in the program in interpreting and in dealing with social and other issues.

Tests used in the Evaluation Survey provide evidence, illustrated in Figure 1, that knowledge and understanding of literature, art, ethics, philosophy and music have been enhanced by the program of humanistic studies. Participants have acquired guides for distinguishing what is significant from what is commonplace and of transient value. They have become more adept in recognizing the origin, nature and significance of literary and artistic trends.

Survey findings, illustrated in Figures 2 and 3, show that participants have acquired better understanding of the forces

[1] H. Thirring, "The Step from Knowledge to Wisdom," *American Scientist* (1956, 44), pp. 445–456.

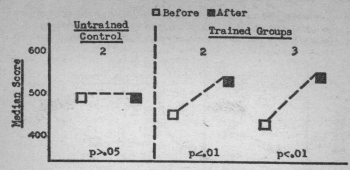

FIG. 1. GRADUATE RECORD AREA TESTS (HUMANITIES)

The *Graduate Record Area Tests* are designed to assess broad outcomes in education in the liberal arts from the sophomore through the first year of graduate study. Part 2, the *Humanities Test*, provides a means of evaluating basic knowledge and understanding in the areas of literature, ethics, philosophy, painting, sculpture, architecture, music and miscellaneous arts.

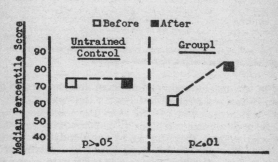

FIG. 2. CO-OPERATIVE GENERAL CULTURE TEST
(HISTORY AND SOCIAL STUDIES)

The *Co-operative General Culture Test* has been widely used to measure achievement of undergraduates in liberal-arts colleges. Part 1, *History and Social Studies*, is designed to appraise "historical perspective," in terms of significant historical facts and of economic and social issues which have appeared in the course of national development, particularly in the Western world. The test was administered only to the *Control* group and *Group 1*.

within the individual and his society which affect the development and operation of a civilization and its institutions. They exhibit increased knowledge of basic concepts and familiarity with contributions of important personalities in the area. More important, test results clearly support the view that participants have acquired increased understanding of the nature and

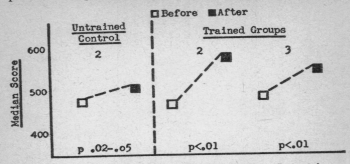

FIG. 3. GRADUATE RECORD AREA TESTS (SOCIAL SCIENCE)

Part 1 of the *Graduate Record Area Tests, Social Science,* covers those phases of nonspecialized education in the social sciences which prepare an individual to understand and deal with the interrelated *social, economic* and *political* problems of contemporary society. The test is constructed on the assumptions that to deal effectively with those problems an individual should: (a) have an understanding of the nature and history of social, economic and political institutions and of the problems arising in relation to them; (b) have the critical abilities necessary to make intelligent use of the materials of social sciences.

history of social, economic and political institutions and of the problems arising in relation to them. In this respect, they have become better prepared to deal with the interrelated social, economic and political problems of contemporary society.

It is also evident, from replies to questionnaires, illustrated in Table 1, that participants have sensed a widening of their social, cultural and ethical horizons in relation to both modern business and personal life. They indicate that they have achieved a better understanding of man and his society, of world issues and pressing problems, and of the role of business in modern society. Such gains can properly be interpreted as movement toward the future "statesmanship" in business which is a concern of the educational program.

A striking finding of attitude research is that increases in knowledge are not necessarily accompanied by significant changes in interests, attitudes, or values. As a result, findings which reveal consistent and statistically significant changes in interests, attitudes and values represent a particularly interesting aspect of the Evaluation Survey.

TABLE 1

Achievement of Educational Objectives: Understanding of Social, Cultural and Ethical Values in Relation to Modern Business and Personal Life

	Average ratings			
	Group 1		Groups 2 & 3	
	Importance	Achievement	Importance	Achievement
Achieving a better understanding of the social and cultural forces affecting modern business	4.6	4.3	4.4	4.4
Understanding world issues and pressing social, political and economic problems.....	4.3	4.5	4.0	4.3
Understanding the meaning and values in life	4.5	4.4	4.3	4.2
Developing a personal philosophy and applying it in daily life........................	4.2	4.2	4.2	3.8
Preparing for a reappraisal of the goals of the business enterprise..................			4.0	3.7
Achieving a better understanding of the role of business in modern society............			4.5	4.2
Learning how to apply ethical and moral values in dealing with the problems of the business organization....................			4.4	3.7

Data presented above were yielded by questionnaires which embodied originally twenty, and in the final form forty, possible *objectives* in the education of an executive. In the analysis of findings, an average *Importance* rating of 4.0 or higher has been considered as indicating that the objective is viewed by program participants as a *highly important* one; an average *Achievement* rating of 4.0 or higher has been considered as indicating that the objective has been *achieved to a large extent*, and an average rating of 3.6-3.9 as representing the opinion that the stated objective has been *adequately achieved*.

Included among such changes are a *ripening of artistic interests* and the *acceptance of aesthetic values* as important guides for judgment and conduct. This is evidenced in findings yielded by the *artistic* scale of the Kuder Preference Record (Figure 4), and also by consistent and significant increases in scores pertaining to the *aesthetic* value, as measured by the Allport-Vernon-Lindzey Study of Values (Figure 5). Questionnaire findings reveal an increased willingness to accept the work of the writer, the artist and the musician as an important contribution to individual and social good. An aura of open-mindedness has crept into the evaluation and even acceptance

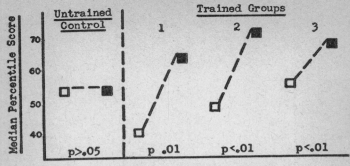

FIG. 4. KUDER PREFERENCE RECORD (ARTISTIC)

The *Kuder Preference Record* measures relative strength of interest in ten broad areas of vocational activity, e.g., *outdoor, mechanical, persuasive, artistic, clerical,* etc. As appears above, each of the trained groups showed upward movement in terms of *artistic* interest. Of the ten scales, only the *artistic* showed consistent change in the same direction for all *Trained* groups.

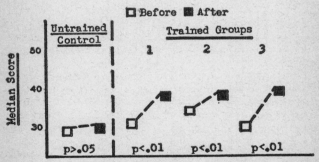

FIG. 5. ALLPORT-VERNON-LINDZEY STUDY OF VALUES (AESTHETIC)

The *Study of Values* was designed to measure the relative prominence of six basic interests or motives in personality, representative of values or evaluative attitudes, based upon Spranger's *Types of Men.* Findings presented above reflect an increasing appreciation of "form" and "harmony," and enhanced "interest in the artistic episodes of life."

of new and "strange" literary styles, artistic patterns and musical tonalities.

Such transformations of aesthetic perceptions are not accompanied by consistent changes in *religious, political* and other

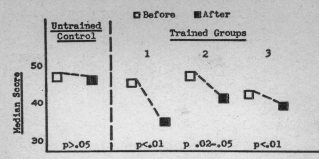

FIG. 6. ALLPORT-VERNON-LINDZEY STUDY OF VALUES (ECONOMIC)

High scores on the *economic* scale of the *Study of Values* are characteristic of men who have deep interest in what is useful. The interest in utilities develops to embrace the practical affairs of the business world. This type is thoroughly "practical" and conforms well to the prevailing stereotype of the average American businessman. The consistent decline in *economic* scores is of particular interest since earlier studies have shown that students of business administration and engineering portray a much higher regard for *economic* value and much less regard for *aesthetic* value than do students specializing in other fields.

values covered by the Study of Values or in areas of interest, other than artistic, included in the Kuder Preference Record. However, as appears in Figure 6, emphasis on the *economic* value appears to decline as aesthetic values acquire greater prominence.

This cannot be interpreted as evidence of a reduced concern for the economic welfare of the business. Thus, questionnaire replies indicate that participants continue to view "making a profit" as a primary goal of a business enterprise. Nevertheless, exposure to the humanities has led participants to attach greater importance to ordinarily neglected values which can contribute to enriched intellectual and emotional perspectives. In this respect, they show movement toward the realization of a major objective of the educational program.

As shown in Figure 7, survey findings also provide indications of movement toward views generally ascribed to the less "conservative" elements of the American population. The Evaluation Survey provides no grounds for the opinion that Bell System executives enrolled in the program are "hidebound conservatives." The best interpretation of the available data is that, as a group, they take the middle of the road on issues of social significance. There is clear evidence, for example, that

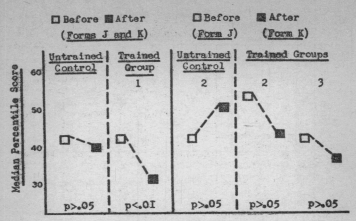

FIG. 7. CONSERVATISM-RADICALISM OPINIONAIRE

The *Conservatism-Radicalism Opinionaire* undertakes to distinguish between those who would "conserve the old" and those who "favor the new." *Conservatism* is represented by high scores on the scale; "striving for new values" or *Radicalism* by low scores.

The questionnaire includes two presumably alternate forms (*J* and *K*), which can be used separately or combined to yield a single score. Both forms were used in *before* and *after* testing of the original *Control* group and of *Group 1*. In the case of *Control 2* and *Group 2* and *3*, *Form J* was used in *before* testing and *Form K* in *after* testing.

Supplementary study of the two forms has shown that the distribution of responses on *Form K* is consistently more in the direction of conservatism than *Form J*, and that the two cannot be considered as truly alternate forms. In part because of this, the data presented above have been viewed as supporting other evidence of movement by participants toward *less* conservative attitudes, although the probability of obtaining the aggregate of the observed differences between *before-after* scores of the *Trained* group is beyond the conventional limits of significance.

they are tolerant of Negroes and of social minorities, and do not take extreme positions in such matters as government interference with business. At the same time, as appears in Table 2, in areas where there is evidence of consistent change in social attitudes, the movement is in the direction of what is ordinarily construed as "liberalism."

As stated earlier, participants have acquired skill in the critical evaluation of significant social, economic, literary, artistic and other issues. However, such skill has little value unless it is accompanied by an increased awareness of the need for carrying on independent thinking as a day-to-day activity. Recogni-

TABLE 2
Social Attitudes

		Per cent					
		Untrained control		Trained groups			
				2		3	
		Before	After	Before	After	Before	After
Individual liberty and justice under law are not possible in socialistic countries...	Disagree	59	53	26	89	48	95
A national economic policy of unrestricted individual enterprise is unsuited to the modern world.......	Agree	18	29	42	79	48	81
As a matter of sound policy, socialism and communism must be viewed as equally evil, since both involve public ownership of means of production....	Disagree	47	47	47	95	76	95
Public interest has made increasing government regulation of the economy a necessity	Agree	41	53	42	68	38	62
Democracy depends fundamentally upon the existence of free business enterprise	Agree	82	94	95	74	90	67
Communism and fascism are basically and historically similar	Disagree	35	41	47	74	57	67

Data presented above are derived from replies to forty items pertaining to issues associated with government and business, world affairs and the social sciences, included in the *Significant Issues Questionnaire* administered to *Control 2* and *Groups 2* and *3*. Items listed above are among those which showed a *consistent* change in the same direction in the case of both *Groups 2* and *3* affecting more than 15 per cent of the combined groups.

tion of this is implicit in the statement that one objective of the educational program is "to offset a tendency to overconformity, which is bound to occur in a business which is highly specialized and which promotes almost entirely from within the organization."

As noted earlier, thoughtful observers of the current American scene contend that it suffers severely from a surfeit of "conformed" as contrasted with "independent" thinking. This, in part, is what David Riesman has in mind in his concept of an "other-directed" society in which judgments and action are based on conformity to the group appraisal of a situation.[2] In such an atmosphere, "behavioral cues no longer come from within, but are taken instead from the peer group." As a result, there appears, especially in lower echelons, a shortage of innovating, self-reliant business leaders and purveyors of economic progress.

A highly significant purpose of the program of humanistic education is to encourage autonomous thinking which is relatively independent of both tradition and group norms, and also enriched by an awareness of forces which have operated in other societies and other civilizations. The Evaluation Survey has furnished considerable evidence of movement away from the practice of conformity in thinking. This is apparent in measures reflecting increased "liberalism" of attitude, to which reference has been made. Scores on the Minnesota T-S-E Inventory provide further evidence of movement toward reflective thought, characterized by freedom from domination by immediate objective conditions and generally accepted ideas. Awareness of increased receptivity to new ideas is reflected in participants' evaluation of the extent to which educational objectives were achieved. Thus, high achievement ratings were assigned to such educational objectives as "reducing the susceptibility of the individual to the influence of emotional propaganda in the field of politics and world affairs" and "developing increased tolerance of different or new ideas." In general, it seems clear that there has been progress toward overcoming that "torpor of conformity in society" which, as seen by Riesman and others, is a basic obstacle to the continuing dynamic development of a vigorous spirit within a capitalistic society.

The findings discussed above provide clear-cut evidence that participants in the program of humanistic education for executives have undergone changes concordant with the goals of the educational activity. It is necessary, however, to recall that the Evaluation Survey was concerned only with the *immediate* and not long-range outcomes of the program. Findings provide no evidence, for example, as to whether participants will "accept the concept of intellectual activity as a never-ending process to be continued throughout the life of the individual" —whether, specifically, they will *continue* to spend time in serious reading, attending concerts, visiting art museums, exploring social and cultural issues, accepting actively their obligations as citizens in the community. Similarly, survey out-

[2] *The Lonely Crowd: A Study of the Changing American Character* (New Haven, Yale University Press, 1950).

comes provide no guarantee that participants will, in such executive posts as they may hold or attain in the future, think and *act* in such a way as to become, in fact, the pioneers of a new "statesmanship in business."

Whether the observed influences of the program after a ten-month period persist and *long-range* goals are achieved can be determined only after a period of years, by follow-up studies of the achievements, activities and views of the individuals participating in the program, in comparison with those who have not had the opportunity to attend the Institute of Humanistic Studies for Executives. Data obtained in a series of interviews with participants at the start of the program provide one basis for such long-range evaluation. Additional techniques have been formulated and preliminary studies already undertaken with a view of assessing the permanence and practical effectiveness of this "bold experiment" in the education of executives. However, only time will give the answer to the questions raised immediately above.

In the meantime, however, consideration of the long-range goals has brought into relief a number of problems which must be faced in the effort to maximize the outcomes of humanistic studies for executives, in terms of effective leadership in the business enterprise. Among these is the problem of facilitating the transfer to the business situation of knowledge, habits of thinking and attitudes acquired during the educational program. There is evidence, both from the Evaluation Survey and other studies, that attitude changes are not readily generalized or easily translated into appropriate decision-making or action in dealing with particular and especially ego-involved situations. Thus, the enhancement of *liberalism*, as reflected in responses to a questionnaire, *may not* carry over to active support or even more ready acceptance of modifications in *specific* cultural patterns or social practices, e.g., nonsegregation.

To the extent that this is true, it becomes necessary to plan the program in such a way as to bridge the gap between *knowledge* and *attitude*, on the one hand, and *action* on the other—to augment the possibility for the effective future motivation and guidance of behavior in the business situation. A step has been taken in this direction in providing what have been called "integration periods" in the current, revised educational program. In these, attention is centered upon an "imaginative" approach designed to help participants to learn to organize the course content and the consideration of values in a meaningful and useful way with respect to business problems; to see more clearly the relationship which course materials and viewpoints have to the business world of today and tomorrow.

It is recognized that this represents only a partial approach, and that much depends upon the receptivity of present management to the implementation of the intellectual horizons, interests, attitudes and thinking habits developed through enrollment in the program of humanistic studies. Research has shown that a training program, such as a human-relations course, may have no beneficial effect unless the supervisor returns to a *management climate* which permits and encourages him to make use of what he has learned. There is every reason to believe that this limitation applies also to a program of humanistic education. There is keen awareness that this represents another problem which must be realistically faced in order to maximize the returns from this "humanistic" approach to the development of a "new statesmanship" in the conduct of the telephone business. Without this, "appearance can displace reality, with dynamism existing only in the claims of apologists and speechmakers."[3]

To say this is merely to raise another problem—that of identifying the characteristics of the satisfactory "management climate." Involved here is the whole question of the fundamental nature of leadership. There is possibly no word which is used more frequently than "leadership" in discussions of the business enterprise by political orators, business managers, and social scientists. There is probably no word in the gamut of verbal clichés which is so loosely defined as is the word "leadership." "Among social scientists," as R. Tannenbaum and F. Massarick have recently pointed out, "the theoretical foundations of leadership have continued to shift, focusing first upon one aspect and then upon another"[4]—from descriptions in terms of supposedly universal traits to analysis in terms of situational functions.

The need for developing a systematic and acceptable theory of leadership is a real one. It is still too early to estimate the extent to which the program of humanistic education for executives will either contribute to the development of such theory or markedly influence the future behavior in industry of participants. However, some comfort can be drawn from a pioneering experiment which reverts to concepts of individuality, of independent thinking, of wide cultural and social perspectives as necessary attributes of business leadership. From a broader point of view, in an era characterized by conformism, which has brought the concept of automation into the study of man himself, it is comforting to find in this program a continuing

---

[3] T. Levitt, "The Changing Character of Capitalism," *Harvard Business Review* (34, 1956), pp. 37–47.

[4] "Leadership, A Frame of Reference," Institute of Industrial Relations, Reprint No. 68 (Los Angeles, University of California, 1958).

consciousness of the individual value and dignity of man—a *denial* of the concept of man as "a servo-mechanism, a behavioristic robot responding helplessly to pinpricks from the environment."[5] Perhaps the chief value of the return to humanistic education is the willingness to do something concrete in the way of turning men in the right direction—in the direction of freedom from that social coercion and those emotional distortions which are at the very root of "creeping conformism" in American life.

russell kirk

The Inhumane Businessman *

AMERICAN BUSINESSMEN ARE INHUMANE. I DO NOT MEAN THAT they are inhuman; they are all too human. I do not mean that they are insufficiently humanitarian. I mean that American businessmen, like most other Americans, are deficient in the disciplines that nurture the spirit. They are largely ignorant of the humanities, which, in a word, comprise that body of great literature that records the wisdom of the ages, and in recording it instructs us in the nature of man. The humanist believes in the validity of such wisdom.

Let us be quite clear about the difference between humanism and humanitarianism. In common usage, humanitarianism has simply come to mean generosity or charity; but strictly defined, as a system of thought, humanitarianism is a belief that mankind can be improved through the application of utilitarian principles, without divine aid; this is the idea that Rousseau pursued ecstatically and Stalin ruthlessly, while they overlooked the human law. Now there are a great many benevolent humanitarians among us who are neither ecstatic nor ruthless. The American businessman by and large is a benevolent humanitarian. In fact, probably no class of businessmen in all history has been so openhanded and so full of social conscience. So I do not mean to say that the American businessman is selfish when I say that he is not humane. But he misunderstands the limited virtues and even the profound hazards of human-

---

[5] J. H. Rush, "The Next 10,000 Years," *The Saturday Review* (January 18, 1958), pp. 11 ff.

* From *Fortune* magazine (May, 1957), copyright 1957 by Time, Inc. By permission of Russell Kirk.

itarianism so long as he neglects, as he does, the wisdom of humanism.

Humanism is a discipline that traces its origins back to the Hebrew prophets and the Greek philosophers, and has existed ever since to *humanize* men. Cicero and Seneca and Marcus Aurelius were at once the Roman exemplars and the Roman preceptors of this humanizing process, for which our term is "a liberal education." The humanists believed that through the study of great lives and great thoughts the minds of earnest men could be molded nobly. The process was both intellectual and ethical. This humane discipline, passed along in the literature of Christian theology, classic philosophy, poetry, history, biography, dominated the thinking of the whole of the Western world—until very late in the nineteenth century. Humanism persists today, but with influence greatly weakened.

The leaders of society in medieval Europe, the landed proprietors and the clergy, were trained in these humane disciplines. And later, the burghers of the Low Countries, the bankers of Lombardy and Tuscany, the manufacturers of England, aspired to know and to patronize humane letters and arts. The founders of the American Republic were practical and bold men; but they also were humane men, influenced by the classic tradition. The model for the American Republic was the Roman Republic, modified by the English political experience; the models for American leadership were Plutarch's heroes.

But with the successive industrial revolutions of the nineteenth and twentieth centuries, with what Friedrich Jünger calls "the triumph of technology," this veneration of humane learning began to disappear—especially among businessmen in America. Applied science, "positivism," seemed to be the keys to complete power. Powerful voices were raised then in disparagement of the humanities and in praise of "efficiency," "pragmatism," "progress." The school of business administration pushed the schools of theology and classical studies into a dim corner. People asked impatiently: Why waste years in school over Cicero?

A people can live upon their moral and intellectual capital for a long time. Yet eventually, unless the capital is replenished, they arrive at cultural bankruptcy. The intellectual and political and industrial leaders of the older generation die, and their places are not filled. The humanitarian cannot substitute for the humane man. The result of such bankruptcy is a society of meaninglessness, or a social revolution that brings up radical and unscrupulous talents to turn society inside out.

The young men who are to govern our industry and, to a considerable extent, our public polity, are in the condition of

Aristotle's slaves, actually disqualified by the necessity of unremitting labor from taking part in public affairs. When they are in their sixties, they may have time for reflection and public service. But there are disadvantages to society in being led by emancipated slaves.

It is not easy to humanize oneself at the age of sixty. And not many businessmen do; the disciplines of humane studies, easily acquired in childhood, are thoroughly tedious in old age. Furthermore, the mortality rate among retired businessmen is notoriously high, perhaps in part because they lack the consolations of philosophy and the relaxation of purely intellectual pursuits.

The pity is that most of our businessmen are unaware of the fact that they are missing anything; they fail to appreciate how much of their intellectual power is wasted in getting and spending. Getting and spending are in themselves generally commendable activities; as Dr. Johnson said, "A man is seldom more innocently occupied than when he is engaged in making money." But that production and promotion should have become the whole of life for so many of the best minds in our country is unjust to the businessman, who deserves a better reward. . . .

Even if the humanities are chiefly important to a man's soul and the higher purposes of life, it ought to be noted they are good for profits, too. One of the ends of a liberal education is to fit a person for whatever lot may happen to be his; and some of the accomplishments of the humane discipline, though that system developed in an age considerably different from ours, are remarkably important to the management of the modern economy.

A person truly educated in the humane tradition should have an orderly and disciplined mind—so far as any system of training can bring order into private personality. He has been taught the relationship between cause and effect. He should understand that predictable consequences follow from particular actions. He has in his mind a fund of precedent. He is acquainted with system. He has been taught a respect for just authority, and that the ego must be kept in check. The complexities of modern business require precisely those habits of thought that a liberal education has been trying to inculcate in young men these several centuries.

The sheer variety of the ideas that the liberal-arts man has explored can be counted upon to give him a resourcefulness generally superior to that of the man who has had only a technical training. Larger possibilities occur to the liberal intellect. Technique, as such, breeds only refinements of existing technique. Imagination rules the world, Napoleon said. Business imagination is not the highest form of imagination; but it certainly rules business in a competitive economy.

It could be argued that a degree in the humanities is even some added guarantee of integrity. The end of the old humanistic schooling, as I mentioned, is ethical: a man seeks virtue through philosophy. There are dishonest intellectuals, just as there are dishonest fools. It is a Latin poet who tells us that a man may perceive the good path and the evil, and yet choose the evil almost against his will, and certainly against his reason; there are no absolute sureties against a fall from virtue. But after reading the philosophers and the prophets and the poets, a man at least must be ashamed of misconduct, for he knows surely what misconduct is.

Liberal education cannot substitute for native shrewdness and knowledge of the ways of the world, but it can supplement and elevate such worldly wisdom. The humane man is able to appreciate human hopes and motives. He has some idea of the complexity and subtlety of the human heart. If he has learned his lessons, he is not likely to think of his own prejudices as universal aspirations, or put a utopian faith in his associates. He probably has taken on a healthy pessimism about the possibilities of human nature. He should know fairly well what may be expected of a man.

He is better prepared to deal with "personnel relations" than the young zealot fresh from courses in Freudian or behavioristic psychology, who immoderately applies the speculations of the clinician to situations and personalities that may require nothing more than a sprinkling of good humor. . . .

We hear a good deal about businessmen in politics, and some of it to the effect that politics is something they have no business being in. Edmund Burke, though he always was supported by the greater part of the industrial and commercial interests of England, did not trust businessmen as statesmen; on one occasion he said that men of commerce were not at all fit to judge of the high concerns of state. The late Robert Taft more than once expressed his annoyance at the notion that the United States needed "a businessman's government." Businessmen, he said, should take care of business, and politicians should take care of politics.

Nevertheless, the businessman does matter in American politics, and he has an important role to play, whether he likes it or not. Many businessmen definitely do not like it; they are busy, and they know when they are out of their element. We hear a lot about the political power of United States business, but the country suffers far more from the political indifference of the businessman than from his alleged political influence. The businessman has to be concerned with our public polity.

Whoever possesses money and influence must play a large role in politics, or else he will not keep money and influence long.

And it is in politics that the businessman without humane disciplines is most conspicuously at a disadvantage. If ignorant of history and political theory and the record of human nature, he may fall victim to the sentimental humanitarian, or worse still, to the zealot for social collectivism. Vaguely eager to be approved by the advanced social thinker, disturbed by denunciations from radical and liberal publications, the inhumane businessman may become a party to his own undoing.

The radical man of action is aware of this weakness of the businessman. More than a generation ago, G. Lowes Dickinson, a British man of letters who happened to be an ardent socialist, informed his friends that they could count upon the conquest of businessmen without a struggle; it would simply entail, said Dickinson, a "slow, half-conscious detachment of all of them who have intelligence and moral force from the interest and active support of their class." The robber barons did some damage in their day; but the possibilities of damage to our social structure by confused and sentimental humanitarians may be even greater.[1]

If businessmen don't assume some political leadership, leaders of a disagreeable and violent sort will make themselves felt in the land. Burke described Jacobinism, the fierce radicalism of France, as "the revolt of the enterprising talents of a country against its property." Jacobinism lies latent in any generation or country. But the possessors of property must be fortified by the councils of humane disciplines. It will do no good for them to flail around in the political arena simply repeating slogans about "the American way of life," or "the American standard of living."

If only by accident, the American businessman has come to be the chief guardian of our civil and cultural inheritance. It is not altogether convenient to have greatness thrust upon one. Yet the American businessman owes it to himself, his economic system and his country to shoulder such responsibilities. I do not expect that any considerable proportion of the business community will set out overnight to read Plato through. We can hope that some of our businessmen will begin to pay some heed to the springs of imagination and reason, and open their minds to our intellectual heritage. Professor Wilhelm Röpke,

[1] A number of our great private charitable foundations are committed not to collectivism, as their adversaries often cry, but to a vague, well-intentioned humanitarianism, looking toward the perfection of society and human nature. Almost any sum of money can be got for almost any "social research project" or plan for material amelioration. But the men running our foundations, taken as a body, seem quite indifferent to the ethical and intellectual premises of the humane tradition.

the Swiss economist and social philosopher, recently suggested that nowhere is the gulf between the man of property and the man of intellect wider than in the United States. This is a perilous condition.

frank w. abrams

The Big Job of the Moment *

UNDERLYING ALL THE PROBLEMS THAT TODAY CHALLENGE US as businessmen, educators, legislators or plain citizens, there is, in my opinion, an over-all challenge or goal—the importance of education to the future of our country and the world through its influence on the behavior of people.

No matter what plans we make, the ultimate test of education is not whether it has succeeded in helping business and industry but whether it has helped to develop better, more rational human beings.

An educational system that turns out, for example, large numbers of highly trained engineers without teaching them how to reason and come to logical conclusions on personal, community, national and world problems, toleration of the rights of others in the working out of the particular problems, and the acceptance of the outcome of a logical conclusion is not education but training. And training is but one aspect—and not the most important one, either—of education. For mere training—even excellent training—does not produce a full man; it may even produce little more than a mechanical, unthinking man. In fact, training without enlightenment may well lead to the type of push-button education characteristic of the large numbers of engineers we hear so much about these days that Russia is turning out.

A free, democratic nation such as ours, with an educational system controlled by its citizens and not by the state, has the moral and practical obligation to the welfare of its people and the stability of its form of government to educate as well as to train.

The educational process that stimulates the ability to reason and project ahead in an orderly fashion the products or conclusions of logical reasoning can, if accomplished in time, have a

* From "A Businessman Looks at Education Past High School," a speech before the President's Committee for Education Beyond High School at New York University, New York, April 30, 1957. By permission of Frank W. Abrams.

beneficial influence on many of our local, national and global problems.

The great problems that exist today, such as, among others, excessive population growth, racial discrimination, juvenile delinquency, loss of individual initiative and the encroachment of government on the private individual, will not be solved by the training of a thousand, or even hundreds of thousands, more engineers and scientists. Unless these men and women, together with others enrolled in our institutions of higher learning, and those that we can influence to continue their education past high school, are given the incentive to learn to think problems through in a logical, tolerant manner, and are willing to accept the conclusions of their thinking, these problems may be left unsolved.

And if this should happen, it may well precipitate action by a centralized authority such as the so-called superstate. It is our job to do what we can to prevent this from happening. But prevention is not enough. We must have a positive and constructive attitude toward our nation's problems, belief in its ideals and faith in its people. And we must formulate our educational programs with this in mind. This, it seems to me, is the big job of the moment for businessmen, for educators, for all of us.

ralph barton perry

When Is Education Liberal? *

A MAN IS FREE, OR HE ENJOYS LIBERTY, IN THE PROPORTION to which his life is governed by his own *choice*. Freedom is not doing as one *pleases*, but doing as one *chooses*. And choice itself is a matter of degree; for it may be wide or narrow, deep or shallow. Choice is narrowed by ignorance, habit or obsession; it is broadened by knowledge, spontaneity and reflection. Choice is also confined by circumstances beyond its control. Choice is vain, or is mere idle wishing, when the chosen is impossible; choice is real and effective when its means lie within its reach. The greater part of human knowledge serves the purpose of making choices effective, whatever they may be. It provides men with tools, and extends their control of cir-

* From *Modern Education and Human Values*, Howard F. Lowry *et al.*, ("Pitcairn-Crabbe Foundation Lecture Series, Vol. III" [Pittsburgh, University of Pittsburgh Press, 1950]). By permission of the University of Pittsburgh Press.

cumstances. Technology and organized industry reduce man's dependence on his physical environment; the social arts reduce his dependence on his social environment. Through these agencies circumstance becomes more plastic to the will; man becomes to a diminishing extent the victim of circumstance, whether the hostile and indifferent forces of nature or his own tyrannies of social custom and authority.

There remains, however, another and a more profound requirement of freedom—that is, of the fullest freedom. Freedom may vary in amplitude—in depth, breadth and range. A man is lacking in freedom in proportion as he is bound by commitments which he has not freely chosen; or he merely chooses means to ends already unconsciously adopted or imposed upon him from beyond himself. A man is lacking in freedom in proportion as his horizon is bounded narrowly. And it is here that liberal education enters the situation.

Education is liberal in so far as it invites and qualifies men to choose deeply and fundamentally, to choose ends as well as means, to choose remote as well as immediate ends, to choose from many rather than from few possibilities. Liberal education, so construed, makes successive generations of men aware of the widest range of possibilities by the discovery of new possibilities, and by reminding of old possibilities forgotten. It does so in order that men may choose with the utmost amplitude of freedom—in order that their lives may be filled to the maximum extent by what they thoughtfully and wittingly choose them to be. . . .

Light is thrown on the meaning of liberal education by naming some of its opposite illiberalities. Liberal education is opposed to a strictly or merely vocational education, or what is better called occupational education, because an occupation, once adopted, narrows the choices that remain open; as a man having adopted the occupation of a physician may then choose only where and how he shall practice. The occupation itself may be imposed by circumstance and livelihood. The physician is then said to have "no alternative" but to practice medicine, or to have "no choice" in the matter. Or the individual, taking into account his capacities and environment, may choose to be a physician, rather than a lawyer, businessman, or artist. His education is then said to be liberal in so far as it acquaints him with these options, and opens the door to them all. Liberal education in this sense properly comes at that period in the individual's life when he has not yet committed himself—at the parting of the ways, like the period when a man is choosing his life partner before he has bound himself, for better or for worse, to anyone. He who chooses his occupation freely, that is, with a comparative awareness and understanding of the possibilities, may then remain free; for if he has no regrets, all the narrower choices to which he is subsequently restricted partake of the freedom of his original and fundamental choice.

Liberal education is opposed to dogmatic education where dogmatic education means the imparting of beliefs without their evidence. In so far as the individual is dogmatically educated his mind submits passively to authority—he takes someone else's word—and does not choose his conclusions by proving their truth for himself. His mind is made up *for* him rather than *by* him.

Merely informative education, which imparts a knowledge of facts, is less liberal than the theoretical education which imparts a knowledge of principles; because he who grasps the principles can then apply and extend them for himself. He is prepared not only for this or that particular actuality but for the infinitude of possibles that are subsumable under general ideas. The grasp of principles creates resourcefulness.

Specialized knowledge is comparatively illiberal because it limits the movement of the mind, and excludes the alternative interpretations of any subject or situation which might be made in the light of a broader context. It also habituates the mind to some specific technique, and so unfits it for dealing with more than one subject matter. . . .

The values which in their sum are comprised within the idea of liberality may be conveyed by any subject matter or educational agency. . . . It will not do, therefore, to say that a professional school is necessarily illiberal because it teaches law or medicine; or because its students are acquiring a special form of expertness for which they expect to be paid, or even because its students are already largely committed to the career. It is quite possible that a law school or medical school should be liberal, and a so-called liberal-arts college be illiberal. . . .

Within the sphere of law a lawyer may choose the branch of law in which he specializes. He may take the law as it is, set down in statutes or in precedents, and merely choose from among its applications to the given situation in which he is called upon for advice; or he may re-examine the law's extra-legal premises, and find reasons why the law is as it is; or he may become a legal reformer. In his legal practice he may be a mere technician, operating on a narrow front; or he may participate in "high policy," and raise his life to the level of strategy and statesmanship. In so far as his legal education has enlarged his outlook, extended the range of possible action, led him back to first principles, taught him how to weigh alternatives, multiplied the means to ends, and the ends which are open to his adoption or rejection, his may be said to have been a liberal education; and his profession may be said to be a liberal profession.

There is no occupational or professional education, whether or not it is called a liberal or learned profession, of which the same may not be said. Education for business is liberal in so far as it teaches a man to choose business for what it is, understanding the role of business in society at large, and in so far as it reveals the underlying principles on which business practice is founded, and enables the business student or businessman to be inventive and creative and not a mere cog in the existing mechanism. Even manual labor partakes of liberality at the moment when a man chooses to work with his hands; or when it becomes a skilled craft requiring taste and invention; or when it is attended with a sense of co-operation and social utility.

As the professional or vocational school may be liberal, so the so-called liberal-arts college may be illiberal, and will be illiberal in so far as it is pervaded with a narrow sectarian bias, or employs methods of mass appeal, or reduces study to the level of drudgery and routine, or otherwise fails to awaken the independent mind and exercise the student in the art of reflective and imaginative choice. . . .

But while there is no subject, by whatever name it is called, that is automatically liberating, there are nevertheless certain studies which, owing to their subject matter, their tradition and the habits and attitudes of those who teach them, are peculiarly apt to be liberating. These, not without reason, are commonly classified as the liberal studies, par excellence: literature and the fine arts, history, religion and philosophy.

If it is asked *why* these studies are liberating, the reason is that they stimulate the imagination, create perspective and breadth of outlook, and thus call into play the faculty of choice. The imagination is the freest of all human faculties. Everything experienced, asserted, proved or done can be *imagined* otherwise. Imagination is the faculty for entertaining possibilities, as yet unrestricted even by the requirements of truth or utility. It is the play of the mind unhampered by either theory or practice. Literature and the fine arts place no restriction on ideas save that they shall be enjoyed in contemplation. Within their wide boundaries they encourage taste, that is, free preference of the best. History frees the mind from bondage to the present and unfolds the wide panorama of civilization in all its ages and types. At the same time it exhibits man's varying fortunes, his successes and failures, and enables him to profit thereby in his choices for the future. Religion should be, although it rarely is, a man's culminating freedom. In his religion he extends his mind to the whole of existence, and to the whole scale of existence, and to the whole scale of values, and establishes an equation between them. The great religious visions present man with ultimate ideals which invite his free adoption.

Philosophy is pledged to transcend every provincialism, of time and space and point of view; and in its special concern with values and their hierarchies assists the mind in ordering its choices. In so far as philosophy is true to its original intent it is *speculative;* that is, it questions assumptions, breaks habits, accepts no "is" without wondering what "it might be," views existence in the context of possibility. "Philosophy," said William James, "is able to fancy everything different from what it is. It sees the familiar as if it were strange, and the strange as if it were familiar. It can take things up and lay them down again. Its mind is full of air that plays round every subject. It rouses us from dogmatic slumber and breaks up our caked prejudices."

Literature, fine arts, history, religion and philosophy—these are the studies which, though they always can be debased to agencies of enslavement, have, as human inquiry is now divided, the largest liberalizing potentiality.

There is, on the other hand, no subject of study whatsoever that may not be illiberally taught or illiberally studied. It should not be forgotten that what is called pedantry was invented in those studies which are commonly classified as liberal. Pedantry is doubly illiberal, in being both deadening to the spirit and useless.

Liberal studies are sometimes given the name of the humanities—a term which is so encrusted with historical and emotional deposits that if it is to clarify the meaning of liberal education, it must be used very guardedly. All parties are agreed, however, that humanities has something to do with man —not man in particular but man in general, the Man in men.

Hence education is humanistic when it invites the attention of different individuals or groups to their common humanity— their common lot within one universe or their common role as citizens of one state and as members of one universal society. Humanistic studies will be fit for all men, and will lie upon a level prior to those differences of circumstance, interest, aptitude and skill by which men take their several places in the social division of labor. Humanistic studies, or studies in so far as they are humane, are good for everybody, and may be said to consist of those studies by which men are made *men,* in advance of being men of any particular kind. Humanistic education so conceived is liberalizing because directly or indirectly it embraces every *human* possibility.

alfred north whitehead

The Aims of Education *

IN THE MODERN COMPLEX SOCIAL ORGANISM, THE ADVENTURE
of life cannot be disjoined from intellectual adventure. Amid
simpler circumstances, the pioneer can follow the urge of his
instinct, directed toward the scene of his vision from the moun-
taintop. But in the complex organizations of modern business
the intellectual adventure of analysis, and of imaginative reconstruction, must precede any successful reorganization. In
a simpler world, business relations were simpler, being based
on the immediate contact of man with man and on immediate
confrontation with all relevant material circumstances. Today
business organization requires an imaginative grasp of the
psychologies of populations engaged in differing modes of
occupation; of populations scattered through cities, through
mountains, through plains; of populations on the ocean, and
of populations in mines, and of populations in forests. It requires an imaginative grasp of conditions in the tropics, and of
conditions in temperate zones. It requires an imaginative grasp
of the interlocking interests of great organizations, and of the
reactions of the whole complex to any change in one of its
elements. It requires an imaginative understanding of laws of
political economy, not merely in the abstract, but also with
the power to construe them in terms of the particular circumstances of a concrete business. It requires some knowledge of
the habits of government, and of the variations of those habits
under diverse conditions. It requires an imaginative vision of
the binding forces of any human organization, a sympathetic
vision of the limits of human nature and of the conditions
which evoke loyalty of service. It requires some knowledge of
the laws of health, and of the laws of fatigue, and of the conditions for sustained reliability. It requires an imaginative understanding of the social effects of the conditions of factories.
It requires a sufficient conception of the role of applied science

* From *The Aims of Education* (New York, The Macmillan Company, 1929), copyright 1929 by The Macmillan Company, copyright
1957 by Evelyn Whitehead, by permission of The Macmillan Company
and Ernest Benn Limited, London; and from *Science and the Modern
World* ("Lowell Lectures" [New York, The Macmillan Company, 1925]),
copyright 1925 by The Macmillan Company, copyright 1953 by Evelyn
Whitehead, by permission of The Macmillan Company and Cambridge
University Press, New York.

in modern society. It requires that discipline of character which can say "yes" and "no" to other men, not by reason of blind obstinacy, but with firmness derived from a conscious evaluation of relevant alternatives. . . .

Another great fact confronting the modern world is the discovery of the method of training professionals, who specialize in particular regions of thought and thereby progressively add to the sum of knowledge within their respective limitations of subject. In consequence of the success of this professionalizing of knowledge, there are two points to be kept in mind, which differentiate our present age from the past. In the first place, the rate of progress is such that an individual human being, of ordinary length of life, will be called upon to face novel situations which find no parallel in his past. The fixed person for the fixed duties, who in older societies was such a godsend, in the future will be a public danger. In the second place, the modern professionalism in knowledge works in the opposite direction so far as the intellectual sphere is concerned. The modern chemist is likely to be weak in zoology, weaker still in his general knowledge of the Elizabethan drama and completely ignorant of the principles of rhythm in English versification. It is probably safe to ignore his knowledge of ancient history. Of course I am speaking of general tendencies; for chemists are no worse than engineers, or mathematicians, or classical scholars. Effective knowledge is professionalized knowledge, supported by a restricted acquaintance with useful subjects subservient to it.

This situation has its dangers. It produces minds in a groove. Each profession makes progress, but it is progress in its own groove. Now to be mentally in a groove is to live in contemplating a given set of abstractions. The groove prevents straying across country, and the abstraction abstracts from something to which no further attention is paid. But there is no groove of abstractions which is adequate for the comprehension of human life. Thus in the modern world, the celibacy of the medieval learned class has been replaced by a celibacy of the intellect which is divorced from the concrete contemplation of the complete facts. Of course, no one is merely a mathematician, or merely a lawyer. People have lives outside their professions or their businesses. But the point is the restraint of serious thought within a groove. The remainder of life is treated superficially, with the imperfect categories of thought derived from one profession.

The dangers arising from this aspect of professionalism are great, particularly in our democratic societies. The directive force of reason is weakened. The leading intellects lack balance. They see this set of circumstances, or that set; but not both sets together. The task of co-ordination is left to those who lack either the force or the character to succeed in some definite career. In short, the specialized functions of the community are performed better and more progressively, but the generalized direction lacks vision. The progressiveness in detail only adds to the danger produced by the feebleness of co-ordination.

This criticism of modern life applies throughout, in whatever sense you construe the meaning of a community. It holds if you apply it to a nation, a city, a district, an institution, a family or even to an individual. There is a development of particular abstractions, and a contraction of concrete appreciation. The whole is lost in one of its aspects. It is not necessary for my point that I should maintain that our directive wisdom, either as individuals or as communities, is less now than in the past. Perhaps it has slightly improved. But the novel pace of progress requires a greater force of direction if disasters are to be avoided. The point is that the discoveries of the nineteenth century were in the direction of professionalism, so that we are left with no expansion of wisdom and with greater need of it.

Wisdom is the fruit of a balanced development. It is this balanced growth of individuality which it should be the aim of education to secure. The most useful discoveries for the immediate future would concern the furtherance of this aim without detriment to the necessary intellectual professionalism.

frederic e. pamp, jr.

Liberal Arts as Training for Executives *

IT IS NOT HARD TO PREDICT THAT THE PRACTICE OF MANAGEMENT will be profoundly affected by the rapidly approaching forces of automation and statistical decision-making.

Any company with a decent regard for its survival must be trying to forecast the terms of those forces, for it must recruit and promote today the executives who will be running the company tomorrow. Can we write the job description for a vice-president of X Manufacturing Company for 1965, or 1975? What will he have to know? What new skills, what new sensitivities will he have to possess to deal successfully with the new

* From "Liberal Arts as Training for Business," *Harvard Business Review* (May-June, 1955). By permission of the *Harvard Business Review*.

elements in management and (what is perhaps more important) the new combinations of old elements?

There have been enough changes just since the end of World
War II to make the job grow alarmingly. . . .

Up to now most of the increased demands on management
have been quantitative. An executive has had to know more
about engineering, about accounting, about his industry, about
the position of his company in the industry, about society and
the world around him—all to the end of better control of
masses of data and information, and better decision-making
on the basis of such material.

Now we are faced with the fact that many of the quantitative aspects of the executive's job are going to recede into the
innards of a computer. Thus, in one company, dozens of clerks
used to work laborious days on their slide rules to provide data
for what were no more than calculated guesses, on top of which
management built a whole pyramid of deliberate decisions. A
computer can now take readings of the whole spectrum of data
at any time desired, give the relevant figures their proper
weights and come up with production schedules, orders for
materials and financial budgets to insure maximum efficiency
of operation.

Nevertheless, the executive is not likely to join the ranks of
the technologically unemployed just because he will have
shucked off many of the problems on which he formerly exer-
cised his executive judgment and "feel." It is inevitable that
new problems will crowd in to take the place of the old ones.
And, in other than quantitative judgments, a new standard
of accuracy and precision will be called for to match the level
of accuracy displayed by the computer. A small fable for executives was played out before millions on television at the 1952
election, when the computer performed faultlessly on faulty
data and came out blandly with answers that could have ruined
a company if they had concerned a gamble on marketing or
capital investment.

In any event, the competitive edge acquired by one company
by acquisition of a computer will not last long in any industry.
Sooner or later all companies will be returned to the equilibrium defined recently by Albert L. Nickerson, president of the
Socony-Mobil Oil Company:

> If one competitor has a material advantage today it—or a
> workable counterpart—is likely soon to become common
> property. An enterprise must rely for survival and progress
> on the personal qualifications of those who make up its
> ranks and direct its destinies.[1]

[1] "Climbing the Managerial Ladder," *Saturday Review* (November 21,
1953), p. 38.

The first question a company must now begin to ask of its candidates for executive responsibility is: What can you do that a computer can't?

In more and more companies, the decisive factor is going to be the breadth and depth of executive judgment. As vast areas of what used to be decision-making become subject to mechanical computations which are all equally correct in all companies, the edge will be won by the company whose executives do a better job of handling the qualitative factors which remain after the measurable factors have been taken out, and then of putting all the pieces together into a single, dynamic whole. . . .

On one point all authorities have agreed. Narrow specialization is not enough; this is already responsible for most of the inability of middle management executives to be considered for promotion. John L. McCaffrey, chairman of the board of International Harvester Company, puts it this way:

> . . . The world of the specialist is a narrow one and it tends to produce narrow human beings. The specialist usually does not see over-all effects on the business and so he tends to judge good and evil, right and wrong, by the sole standard of his own specialty.
>
> This narrowness of view, this judgment of all events by the peculiar standards of his own specialty, is the curse of the specialist from the standpoint of top management consideration for advancement. Except in unusual cases, it tends to put a roadblock ahead of him after he reaches a certain level.[2]

Thus, there has been a growing call for "breadth" in educational preparation for management, and a surprising degree of agreement on the need for more *liberal arts* in colleges. . . .

Viewed in these terms many subjects and disciplines can lay claim to a role in education for management. It is obvious that wider subject matter, more courses about more things in the contemporary world, will give the student more breadth.

But it is also apparent that in a day when the executive will be able to dial the electronic reference library and get all the facts about all the subjects he wants, mere accretion of facts will not warrant his putting in the time to prepare merely to know more facts. The call is for more than breadth alone; it is for the ability to move surely and with confidence on unfamiliar ground, to perceive central elements in situations and see how their consequences fall into line in many dimensions. Tomorrow's executive must be able to move surely from policy to action in situations that will be different from anything any generation has experienced before.

There have been developments in traditional educational

[2] *Fortune* (September, 1953), p. 129.

disciplines within the liberal arts which, much to the surprise of those closest to them, will very likely turn out to be far more important to educational preparation for management than many of the flashy subjects that have seemingly been set up to serve business' needs exclusively. The study of the *humanities* —of literature, art and philosophy, and of the critical terms that these disciplines use to assess the world—is startlingly more pertinent and practical than the "practical" vocational preparation.

These disciplines have of course other axes to grind than preparing executives to fill job descriptions. They are elements in our civilization which give it life beyond any technologies or economic systems. The arts, education and management all serve a higher purpose, and business will do society no good if it demands, as do some business leaders, that education serve business directly and solely. That would be the same as insisting that a corporation be restricted only to working capital and forbidden to raise long-term funds.

But the very fact that the humanities serve a larger need than management training is one of the main reasons why they are so valuable for that purpose.

At first glance, the importance of training in these fields hitherto considered peripheral, if not downright irrelevant, to management may be difficult to see. The contribution of the physical sciences is obvious. Also, at long last, we have come to appreciate the significance of the social sciences, which appear to relate directly to business both because of their content and because of their disciplines. It is obvious that an executive must be able to interpret the social and political environment in which his company operates. Further, he must be familiar with as much of the growing body of knowledge of human behavior as possible. But the liberal arts have always been considered remote from the practical hurly-burly of daily decision-making.

To demonstrate that precisely the reverse is true, let us examine the disciplines within which the executive moves. In so doing, we may alter our ideas of his job as it has traditionally been regarded, and bring into focus the parallels between the disciplines of the liberal arts and the disciplines of management.

If we analyze the central activity of the executive, his *process of decision,* we can see three kinds of disciplines which prepare directly for the skills and qualities needed:

(1) The executive must distinguish and define the possible lines of action among which a choice can be made. This requires imagination, the ability to catch at ideas, shape them into concrete form and present them in terms appropriate to the problem.

(2) He must analyze the consequences of taking each line of action. Here the computer and operations research techniques can do much, but the executive must set the framework for the problems from his experience and imagination, and work with his own sensitivity and knowledge in the area of human beings where statistics and scientific prediction are highly fallible guides.

(3) Then in the decision he must have the grasp to know its implications in all areas of an organism which is itself far from being absolutely predictable: the company, the market, the economy and the society. . . .

In view of all this, what can the humanities offer that is pertinent to the executive's job? For one thing, there is plenty of testimony that a common factor in executive success is the ability to express oneself in language. To illustrate:

> There have been many examinations of the background of executives to discover the secrets of success, which have pointed to other than technical accomplishments. In the most recent of these, by Wald and Doty in this magazine, which is more an examination in depth than any that have gone before, it is clear that the literary aptitude of the 33 executives examined was high compared to the scientific. These executives also felt that English was one of the most useful subjects they could take in college to help them toward success.[3]

It is certainly true that the student in the humanities goes deeper into language, and must get more from it and do more with it. But to assume from this that language is only a tool is to stop far short of the possibilities.

Language is not only a tool; it is the person himself. He makes his language, but his language also makes him. "Speak that I may know thee" is the old saw. Any study of language that stops with "techniques of communication," that sees the relationship as one-directional, is stunting the student's growth as an individual. Thus the study of literature as communication only, and not also as experience, is short-changing the student. Study of literature for its own sake is an activity which widens and deepens the personality.

Arthur A. Houghton, a director of Corning Glass, poses the problem bluntly with his statement opening a College English Association Conference at Corning:

> The executive does not deal with physical matter. He deals exclusively with ideas and with men. . . . He is a skilled and practical humanist.

[3] Robert M. Wald and Roy A. Doty, "The Top Executive—A First-hand Profile," *Harvard Business Review* (July-August, 1954), p. 45.

Human situations are controlling in a large proportion of business decisions. The executive, it is agreed, must be able to deal with these situations before all else. The instincts for plucking out the fullest implications and keys to human situations are not developed in technical courses of study, nor even in courses in human relations where the techniques pragmatically set the key for action.

There are numerical keys to situations, from accounting; there are quantitative keys, provided by operations research and other techniques drawn from the physical sciences; there are theoretical keys, such as those of Freudian analysis; and there are the keys of the social sciences, which claim to have no preconceptions or assumptions but which are guided by doctrines nonetheless. But none of these keys provides the executive with the ability to see situations as a whole after and above all the data that are available, to seize on the central elements and know where the entry of action can be made.

The fullest kind of training for this ability can actually be given by the practice of reading and analyzing literature and art. In his function the executive must do pretty much what a critic of literature must do, i.e., seize upon the key, the theme of the situation and the symbolic structures that gives it life. The executive must, moreover, create his object for analysis by himself, combining the ingredients of people and data. He must develop insight of an analytic, subjective kind—something he will never get in terms of pure science, for people and things in management situations just will not behave themselves with the admirable regularity and predictability of gases in a test tube!

The fact is, of course, that science itself has had to reconsider its assumptions about the nature of creative activity in its own field. In place of the mechanical concept of the mind as a computer, patiently turning over the whole range of possible solutions one by one until it lights on the right one, explanations of scientific discovery now sound more and more like artistic or literary creation. . . .

The creative element in management, as in the humanities, is developed by the disciplined imagination of a mind working in the widest range of dimensions possible. Some of those dimensions can be more precisely stated. As Clarence Randall has put it:

> My job today is in the realm of ideas. If I must delegate, I must delegate the things that are physical; the things that are material. . . .[4]

[4] Waller Carson, Jr., "Looking Around: Management Training," *Harvard Business Review* (March-April, 1953), p. 144.

Many others have agreed that the most valuable commodity in management is ideas. Yet those disciplines which explore ideas for their own sake, which treat ideas as having life and interaction of their own, have been set off by many as "impractical." Now that the range is widening for management problems, we shall do well to demand that the traditional disciplines, which have dealt in ideas as they interact, in situations as wide as the artist's view of life, become a major part of education for managers. The greater this range of resource for the minds of management, the more and better will be the ideas that emerge.

Because literature is the disciplined control and development of ideas, it deserves a prominent place in this educational plan. Furthermore, to deal with literature and the arts is to deal with ideas not in the stripped and bloodless way of science, but in the inclusive, pell-mell way that experience comes to us in real life—ideas and practice all muddled up.

Lyndall F. Urwick, in a lecture given a few years ago at the University of California, said:

> What the student needs is a universe of discourse, a frame of reference, so that when he encounters the raw material of practical life his mind is a machine which can work fruitfully upon that material, refer his own practical experience, which must be extremely limited, to general principles, and so develop an attitude, a guiding philosophy, which will enable him to cope with the immense responsibilities of business leadership in the twentieth century.

The executive's job, like life, is just one thing after another. The executive must be continually and instinctively making order and relation out of unrelated ideas—sorting, categorizing—to the end of action. The order he is able to impose on this mass of experience and the actions he initiates determine his success as an executive. He must find meanings for his company and his function, not only in control reports, balance sheets, market data and forecasts, but also in human personalities, unpredictable human actions and reactions; and he must refer all to a scale of values. He must be prepared to answer the demand of the people who work for him: that their work contribute to the meaning of their lives. Without some awareness of the possibilities for meaning in human life, he is not equipped for this central job of managing people. That awareness is a direct function of the humanities.

The key to the executive's situation and problem, then, is the fact and type of the network of meanings he must use and deal with. They are his stock in trade. He must remain aware of significance and meaning in the obvious: production rates, standards, absenteeism and the rest. But today he must be acquiring more awarenesses to keep up. These can no longer be limited to the political and international. They are wider. Here the experience and criticism of the arts—especially literature—are direct preparation; for reading of this kind is above all a search for meanings. The mind that leads this search in literature and art—the author, the artist, the composer—is the most sensitive and aware. The mind that follows—the reader, the listener, the viewer—is itself stretched in the process; it, too, is going to grow more alert and aware.

Meanings on the widest possible level feed perception on a narrower one. The executive whose experience of meanings is thus widened has a suppleness of perception on narrower problems which can key them to effectiveness and co-ordination with policies and objectives on up the scale of management.

It is only prudent, then, that the executive's preparation include a participation (actual or vicarious) in the highest development of this process. Every novel and play and poem is an imposition of order in terms of human beings and of meaning in terms of a scale of values on the elements of experience that are found formless and pointless in any human experience. The terms by which this order is achieved over the whole scale of management action uses technology and science as tools, but it must have a sense of the whole and of values to be fully effective.

One of the most perceptive comments on the nature of the executive's job was made by Crawford H. Greenewalt, president of Du Pont:

> . . . The basic requirement of executive capacity is the ability to create a harmonious whole out of what the academic world calls dissimilar disciplines.[5]

This ability to see the whole of things is again a central function of the humanities. The sciences have flourished by acute concentration upon those elements of the universe that can be measured, but science itself will today admit that it is not a means to the knowledge of the whole of man or of the universe.

The whole of a play or a poem or a novel is the object of the studies of literature because the meaning and structure of each part of it make sense only in terms of the whole. Thus one can say that this feeling for completeness which must govern management even more in the future than it has in the past is directly served by the humanities.

Another, and perhaps the most important, aspect of the executive's job is the fact that he must operate in terms of

[5] "We Are Going to Need More Executives," *Chemical and Engineering News* (May 25, 1953), p. 2173.

values. Peter F. Drucker puts this at the center of the management job:

> Defining the situation always requires a decision on objectives, that is, on values and their relationship. It always requires a decision on the risk the manager is willing to run. It always, in other words, requires judgment and a deliberate choice between values.[6]

Only in the humanities are values inextricable from the materials that are studied. The significance of this is pointed up by a comment in the Yale Report on General Education:

> The arts are distinguished by the fact that their order already exists in the material studied. . . . The student who works with them learns to deal with intuitive symbolic ways of interpreting experience, ways which combine into one order the rational, the descriptive and the evaluative.[7]

If there is a better description of the basic elements of management decision than that last sentence, I have not seen it. Men who must deal with situations above all in terms of values must be prepared by being exposed to those disciplines which admit that they are the stuff of all human life. It is here, too, that the most obvious reason usually advanced for the advantage of the humanities to an executive gains a new significance. With this equipment he is more likely to have interests outside the business. Not only is he thus likely to be less feverishly possessive about his status in the company, but he has available a far more extensive range of values against which to set his relations with others in the company and the policies of the company itself as well (when he is in a position to set those policies). . . .

Those disciplines in education which provide human and traditional perspective on the sciences and social sciences have always been of the highest importance in developing this ultimate management skill; they will become more important as time goes on, for, as President Nathan Pusey of Harvard has remarked, "The humanities draw things back together."

The essence of the humanities, then, is meanings and value judgments on all levels. When they are well taught, they force the student to deal with things as a whole, with the gradations and expressions of meaning, worked out in terms of experience co-ordinated by values and communicated by the disciplined imagination of the artist or writer. These meanings, in a framework of fact, intellect, emotion and social values, are pulled together in an essentially spiritual complex.

[6] "On Making Decisions," *Dun's Review and Modern Industry* (August, 1954), p. 27.

[7] "Report of the President's Committee on General Education," mimeographed (New Haven, 1953), p. 15.

The key to management, and to the executives who make it up, is found in its very nature as an activity. It is easy to define management as a combination of resources, but the fact that the human resources in that combination are in a very special way unique is something that links the humanistic disciplines and management far more firmly than engineering links production to science. . . .

Participation as a student in the poetic process of turning vision into rhetoric is parallel basically to the central problem of the executive, when he works to get policy and company goals into action, integrating plans and objectifying them. And executive action in its own way is no less an art.

There are levels of organization in intellectual disciplines as well as in people. On the level of composition, rhetoric and communication the humanities offer useful tools for the technician in business. But there also are higher levels of organization and integration in work of literary art, which correspond to the integrated personality for which management is looking. Only by exposure to these can we hope to get the character which is essentially the organization of the personality on the highest level of values.

To neglect the humanities in education is to accept the doctrine of the educationalists as set by John Dewey: "The educational process has no end beyond itself." Management has already discovered that the corporation cannot long exist if it has no end beyond itself. It has now seen its error in giving education the impression that the end of education should be the service of the technical needs of business. There is a new synthesis now in the making through which the true ends of both can best be served. It remains only for management to put it into effect.

james c. zeder

Stability in an Era of Change *

I FIRMLY BELIEVE THAT IT WOULD BE BENEFICIAL TO ALL CONcerned—the college, the student, and the employer—if the hardware, plumbing and wiring in today's undergraduate engineering curriculum were reduced drastically or eliminated altogether. The four-year curriculum should not waste the student's

* From "Educating the Individual for a Changing World," an address before the Thomas Alva Edison Foundation's Fourth Annual Children's Book Luncheon, New York, February 3, 1959. By permission of James C. Zeder and the Edison Foundation.

time by teaching him specialized techniques that are certain to become obsolete. Instead, it should provide him with the scientific and engineering fundamentals that will prepare him to meet new challenges—to explore new frontiers—and to tackle new jobs. It should teach him to look beyond his slide rule to the needs of men and nations. And it should give him the ability to relate his work to the advancement of the human community.

I have found widespread agreement among educators, business executives and professional men that education in other professional fields should have similar aims and objectives. Just recently I had the privilege of chairing a series of four conferences attended by twenty of the nation's educational leaders. These conferences were held to obtain the best possible advice in preparing a curriculum for a separate university which is being established by Michigan State University in Oakland County, near Detroit.

The panelists included some of the greatest names in contemporary American education, such as Sarah Blanding, president of Vassar; Lee DuBridge of the California Institute of Technology; Milton Eisenhower of Johns Hopkins; and Carroll Newsom, of New York University. . . . The panelists were asked how they would organize an educational program at this new college, which will not be hampered by traditions and already established educational policies. To promote a free exchange of ideas, their remarks were not recorded verbatim. But discussion in each of the conferences was summarized. I would like to quote briefly from some of these summaries.

The summary of the conference on education for business said:

> It has become increasingly clear that it is not the function of undergraduate education to train a businessman, but to produce a citizen and an educated human being. While it is true that the student should be provided with orientation toward his vocation, it is truer still that any curriculum that attempts to provide at the undergraduate level the skills and knowledge which the mature businessman has at his disposal is destined to failure. Such a curriculum totally ignores the complexity of business and the nature of change in a dynamic society. . . . Would it not be wiser to devote the entire four years to teaching students of business how to understand society, to reason well, and to develop imagination and creativity? . . .

The summary of the conference on the liberal arts stated:

> There exists in the liberal arts a body of knowledge, of skills and of attitudes which *all* students of collegiate grade should master or at the very least should be exposed to.

The panelists agreed that, in general, liberal-arts education should be directed toward developing in all students

> the ability to communicate with precision and at a level of some profundity . . . a knowledge of the past . . . an understanding of the nature of science as an intellectual process . . . and the ability to think creatively and critically. . . .

They recognize that the demands of our nation for professionally trained men and women—for scientists, teachers, doctors, engineers and administrators—show no signs of slackening. But they recognize, too, that professional education must go beyond specialized technical knowledge alone—that it must extend into the broad understanding, insight and perspective which have been historically associated with *liberal* education. They recognize that the business executive, the engineer, the doctor, the scientist need to understand the world's social and political problems, as well as its economic and technical problems, and that they must be aware of the cultural and humanistic values upon which our society rests.

There are other considerations, of course, in developing the imaginative, creative men and women our country must have. We need a greater emphasis on the fundamental arts and sciences at the secondary-school level. We need to give considerably more attention to identifying and educating individuals of unusual talent or potentialities. We need a greater realization that education must begin and continue in the home. And we need to recruit more and abler people into all sectors of the teaching profession.

It seems to me, however, that in order to be really effective in our preparation for the challenges of a rapidly changing world we may have to go one step further—or one fathom deeper—in our thinking about education. We may need to go beyond all the specifics of curriculum content and teaching methods to the *spiritual and psychological needs of human beings*. No man is just a thinking machine or a bundle of skills or a filing cabinet of ideas. What we need to remember is that in man's nature there is a spark that ignites his creative energies and makes him a useful, responsible and effective person. Perhaps there has been a tendency to take this too much for granted. Perhaps we need a greater realization that it is the responsibility of education to develop this spark in as many young men and women as possible.

In this connection, it seems to me, we should consider what effect the forces and pressures of this changing technological age are having on the human personality. In recent years we have been hearing from many writers and commentators that our society is sick with the disease of conformity. We are told that our young people are simply a herd of rock-and-roll fans; that group-mindedness in business and government is creating a nation of organization men and destroying the initiative and vigor of American business enterprise; that team action is stifling scientific invention; that what we need is more people schooled in the tenets of rugged individualism.

It is my belief that those who are drawing this dismal picture of modern life are guilty of oversimplification. They are trying to make black and white distinctions where, in fact, there are none to be made. They overlook the many conditions of our day that make teamwork and common effort necessary.

Big and complex operations in business, research, government and international affairs require the effective combination and utilization of *many* skills and abilities. In a world of constantly expanding knowledge, no man can be an island unto himself—unless it is an extremely small and perhaps insignificant island. And we can expect that the vast enterprises and growing challenges of the future will demand, more than ever, a pooling of talents, a meeting of minds, and a concert of opinion.

However, some of the critics may have touched upon something that is vital and fundamental. There may be some truth in what they say. Perhaps too often we have tried to huddle together, to plan by committee, to organize a team, in order to avoid the responsibility and loneliness of individual thought and decision. Maybe we have acquired too much distaste for uniqueness and individuality. Perhaps in too many cases we have tried to replace individual imagination and creation with brain-storming and group action.

Certainly the contemporary world needs men who know how to make creative contacts with other men, who know how to motivate and lead others, who know how to co-ordinate and co-operate—yes, even in committees. But isn't it possible that what we need *most* is individuals who can remain stable in an exceedingly unstable world, who have the spiritual rudders to maintain their course in the rough seas of the turbulent twentieth century? Isn't it possible we need individuals who have moral conviction, lofty ideals and personal pride and confidence —men and women who have individual integrity and who always retain that integrity in dealing with others?

If this is true, then it is also true that we should consider *how our schools and universities can best cultivate the individual's deepest mental and spiritual qualities; how education can give him the creativity, the inner direction, the stability he needs in an era of dynamic and often violent change.* Though it is not easy to say precisely how this can be done, I am sure it *cannot* be accomplished by limiting one's education to a narrow professional or technical specialty. I am certain that basically it is a job for the branches of knowledge that are concerned with the farthest reaches of the human spirit—religion, of course, but also philosophy, history, literature, the fine arts, psychology and sociology.

These are the studies that give a man the ability to evaluate change in terms of human progress, that prepare him to accept new discoveries without discarding the valid experiences of the past. These are the studies that give him the understanding and motivation that make for a creative life and for creative work. These are the studies that prepare him to make wise and sure decisions. . . .

peter f. drucker

The Importance of Language *

THE MANAGER HAS A SPECIFIC TOOL: INFORMATION. HE DOES not "handle" people; he motivates, guides, organizes people to do their own work. His tool—his only tool—to do all this is the spoken or written word or the language of numbers. No matter whether the manager's job is engineering, accounting or selling, his effectiveness depends on his ability to listen and to read, on his ability to speak and to write. He needs skill in getting his thinking across to other people as well as skill in finding out what other people are after.

Of all the skills he needs, today's manager possesses least those of reading, writing, speaking and figuring. One look at what is known as "policy language" in large companies will show how illiterate we are. Improvement is not a matter of learning faster reading or public speaking. Managers have to learn to know language, to understand what words are and what they mean. Perhaps most important, they have to acquire respect for language as man's most precious gift and heritage. The manager must understand the meaning of the old definition of rhetoric as "the art which draws men's heart to the love of true knowledge." Without ability to motivate by means of the written and spoken word or the telling number, a manager cannot be successful. . . .

It can be said with little exaggeration that of the common

* From *The Practice of Management* (New York, Harper & Brothers, 1954). By permission of Peter F. Drucker and Harper & Brothers.

college courses being taught today the ones most nearly "vocational" as preparation for management are the writing of poetry and of short stories. For these two courses teach a man how to express himself, teach him words and their meaning and, above all, give him practice in writing.

john ciardi

An Ulcer, Gentlemen, Is an Unwritten Poem *

THE POET IN OUR TIMES IS A FIGURE OF ESTRANGEMENT AND he knows it. He not only knows it, he has grown used to the fact and does not much mind it. The truth seems to be, for that matter, that the poet—outside those golden ages of folk poetry now long gone—never did reach more than a few special people in any culture.

In the past, however, poets have managed to persuade themselves that they were some sort of social force. Elizabethan poets liked to claim that their sonnets conferred immortality on the ladies they wrote about. The seventeeth-century satirists were especially fond of the idea that by "holding folly up to ridicule" they purified the intellect of their ages. More recently Shelley found it possible to assert that "Poets are the unacknowledged legislators of the world." And even within the last twenty-five years, the social poets of the thirties may be cited as having seriously believed that their poems of social protest had a measurable effect on the government of nations.

Stephen Spender, looking back on the mood of poetry in the thirties from the vantage point of 1950, summarized the poet's then-sense of himself as very much a warrior of the practical world:

> It was still possible then to think of a poem as a palpable, overt, and effective anti-fascist action. Every poetic assertion of the dignity of the individual seemed to be a bullet fired in the war against human repression.

I know of no sane poet today who persuades himself that the action of his art and imagination has any significant conse-

* From *Canadian Business* (June, 1955). By permission of John Ciardi.

quence in the practical reality of Dow-Jones averages, election returns and state of the nation. Wherever the practical world may be, Auden has defined the position of poetry in our time:

> For poetry makes nothing happen: it survives
> In the valley of its saying where executives
> Would never want to tamper; it flows south
> From ranches of isolation and the busy griefs,
> Raw towns that we believe and die in; it survives,
> A way of happening, a mouth.

But no—perhaps to prove that poets are no prophets—the executives have wanted to tamper. Under the auspices of the College English Association a group of leading business executives have been meeting regularly with writers and teachers of the liberal arts, and from their problems in the practical world of business management, they seem to be asking seriously what meeting there can be between the arts and the practicalities of industry.

The answer to these questions may well be that the poets and the practical men would be mutually happier in leaving one another strictly alone, the poets on their ranches of isolation practicing a way of happening, and the practical men in their cities of numbered and lettered glass doors busily pushing the buttons of the world.

For the gap that divides the poet from the practical man is real. Nor will it be measurably closed by pointing out that some men have functioned with distinction in both the poetical and the practical imagination. There was a director of public works named Chaucer, there was a bricklayer named Ben Jonson, there was a good soldier named Richard Lovelace—one could compile endlessly. But all that such a list would prove is that some men are ambidextrous; it would not eliminate the distinction between the right hand and the left.

A poem is a kind of human behavior. Plowing a field, running a chemical experiment and analyzing the character of a job applicant are also kinds of human behavior. The poem may, of course, be about any one of these human actions; but when the poem deals with them, it does so in nonpractical ways. The poet who writes about plowing a field may find significance in the *idea* of plowing, or he may describe plowing so richly that the riches of the description become a self-pleasing idea in themselves. He does not, however, turn physical soil, plant an actual crop and take it to the literal human diet by way of a negotiable cash market. In the same way, the poet may create a powerfully penetrating picture of the character of the man the business executive is interviewing for a job. But when the poet has finished his analysis, he has no need to make a pay-roll decision and to assign the man to a specific job in a specific department.

Poetry and practicality are in fact two different worlds with two different workers of experience and of imagination. The poet enters his world as an *as if:* he writes *as if* he were analyzing a real man seated before him. He is free with a stroke of the pen to change the lineaments of the world he has imagined. The work sheets of a poem by Karl Shapiro contain a monumental example of this freedom to *as if* at will.

Setting out to describe the [*as if*] dome of darkness that settles over a city at night, he writes in his first draft: "Under the fatherly dome of the universe and the town." Now "fatherly dome" cannot fail to imply a theoretical universe in the mind of God the Father. For reasons that need not be examined here, Shapiro, in his second draft, rephrased the idea "under the dome of zero." Simply by changing one central word, Shapiro swung the universe itself from the theological concept of "father" to the scientific concept of "zero." And the poem continued to follow itself as if the process of reversing thirty centuries of human attitudes in a single word amounted to nothing whatever.

The practical man has no such large freedom. He enters a world called *is*. When he is at work, he *is* plowing a field, he *is* assembling chemical apparatus, he *is* interviewing an actual man whose name appears on the census listings and who *is* offering his services in return for real and taxable wages.

It is only natural, moreover, that men who give their attention to either of these two worlds should not be especially well disposed to the other. Poets tend to think very little of stock-brokers, and stockbrokers tend to think even less—if at all—of poets. And the fact is that some of the best poetry of our times has been written on what may be called an inverted sense of reality, an order of imagination that asserts openly or by implication that what the practical men do is meaningless and that only the *as if* of the vicarious imagination has a place in the final mind of man. So Wallace Stevens, in a poem significantly titled "Holiday in Reality," listed a series of things seen and said of them: "These are real only if I make them so," and concluded: "Intangible arrows quiver and stick in the skin/ And I taste at the root of the tongue the unreal/ Of what is real."

It may be very much to the point that Wallace Stevens, in another part of his imagination, was a vice-president of the Hartford Accident and Indemnity Company and a specialist in claims on surety bonds. Obviously, however, Wallace Stevens

could not look into his surety-bond claims and send in a report
that "These are real only if I make them so." That difference
between the world of practical solutions and the world of the
vicarious imagination must not be blinked away.

What must be borne in mind, rather, is the fact that no sane
human being is exclusively a practical man. The plant manager
may be the most mechanically efficient of calculators during
his waking hours; and still his dreams or his nightmares will be
human and impractical. What is his order of reality and of
business efficiency when he first holds his newborn child? Or
when, as some men must in time, he stands by his child's grave?
What is his order of reality when he steps out of a late conference and finds a hurricane shaking the earth? Or his wife is ill
and the telephone rings: In one ear he hears his assistant
howling that the subcontractor sent the wrong parts and that
a rush order is delayed, while with the other he hears the doctor
close the bedroom door and start down the stairs to tell him
his wife will or will not recover. Which of these realities is
more real than the other to live to?

The poem does not care and cannot care what happens to
that rush order. The poem is of the humanity of the man. And
despite the tendency . . . [to admire] only those men who "do
things" and to scorn "dreamers," the fact is that no man can
be wholly practical or wholly impractical, and that the humanity of any man's life requires some, at least, of both orders of
the imagination.

There is no poetry for the practical man. There is poetry
only for the mankind of the man who spends a certain amount
of his life turning the mechanical wheel. But let him spend too
much of his life at the mechanics of practicality and either he
must become something less than a man, or his very mechanical efficiency will become impaired by the frustrations stored
up in his irrational human personality. An ulcer, gentlemen,
is an unkissed imagination taking its revenge for having been
jilted. It is an unwritten poem, a neglected music, an unpainted
water color, an undanced dance. It is a declaration from the
mankind of the man that a clear spring of joy has not been
tapped, and that it must break through, muddily, on its own.

Poetry is one of the forms of joy, the most articulate, the
most expanding, and, therefore, the most fulfilling form. It is
no separation from the world; it is the mankind of the world,
the most human language of man's uncertain romance with the
universe.

frederic r. gamble

Communications and Distribution*

ESSENTIALLY, SELLING AND ADVERTISING CONSIST OF COMMUNI-
cating information and persuasion. This requires high talents
of the human mind and the understanding of human nature.
Some people seem to be born with these gifts; others acquire
them.

There is general agreement among experienced communica-
tors that the best background is one of history, sciences, languages, economics, social studies, including nowadays new
studies of human motivations—the kind of formal training
usually described as liberal arts. . . .

In recent years some academic leaders have lamented the
decline of liberal-arts education and have sought to revive it by
advocating liberal arts for individual enjoyment or for the
development of the complete man. These benefits of liberal arts
are, no doubt, true today as they always have been, but I believe liberal-arts education has a greater future than it has
ever had.

American business has been learning and using the values
of liberal arts. I believe American business will turn more and
more to liberal arts for the talents it will need in distribution,
just as it turns to the sciences and technical schools for the
talents in production.

It seems to me almost certain that a great expansion of
liberal-arts education lies immediately ahead.

a. m. sullivan

The Aristocracy of Intellect †

WHETHER OR NOT OUR PRESENT BUSINESSMAN IS THE CONVER-
sational equal or superior of his forebears may be a subject of
prolonged debate, but the businessman of the nineteenth century wrote a better letter than the twentieth-century businessman for several reasons. He frequently composed by hand and

* From "Distribution and the Liberal Arts College," Knox College
Commencement Address, June 10, 1957. By permission of Frederic R.
Gamble.

† From *The Three-Dimensional Man* (New York, P. J. Kenedy &
Sons, 1956). By permission of A. M. Sullivan and P. J. Kenedy & Sons.

recopied his message in order to have a file copy. His choice of language reflected the time given to reading and his care in getting precise meanings. He avoided the flat phrases of the mental pauper and the repetitions of the intellectual parrot.

If we gather a week's incoming mail, we can observe how few letters contain the original idea, the shrewd avoidance of commercial cliché, the verbal enterprise of the man with a reasonably large inventory of words and phrases that are not frayed with repetition. A good secretary can often put some variety into hackneyed observations, but few correspondents have any subtlety, even in the use of invective or irony. There is an opportunity for improvement in the amenities and courtesies not only of the commercial letter but also in personal correspondence. The typewriter, the antidote to writer's cramp; the telephone, the excuse of the man too lazy to write; the telegraph, the device of the man who mistakes brevity for clarity, reduce man's urge to leisurely self-expression.

The nineteenth-century European, through the eyes of Charles Dickens, looked upon the American businessman as a precocious, bumptious and ill-mannered child. The twentieth-century European holds to some of these opinions but is willing to temper his criticism. The apparent immaturity of the American is compensated for by a boisterous and generous spirit. He meets his problems with an energy and confidence that jar the cynicism of the European and occasionally win his admiration. . . .

. . . The American businessman cannot quote classical poetry like the Briton, and his familiarity with music is seldom equal to that of the Frenchman or Italian. He deals usually in opposites—black and white, right and left, good and bad. Distinctions to him are often evasions in which the disputant lacks the courage of his convictions. His faith is a shining shield unblemished by despair. Lacking an ancient tradition, he borrows a synthetic and composite coat of arms: the plow and ax crossed with a mule rampant. He has no roots in failure, and if his civilization is unduly influenced by the measure of material things, his ethical standards are high and his cultural standards are showing a slow gain in his resistance to the compression of mass education and mass entertainment. . . .

. . . The man who can lay aside the problems of the day for a few hours of adventure in a library, a gallery, wandering through a ghetto or under a porous umbrella of stars returns to his desk or bench with a livelier step for the tasks at hand. The liberal art is the badge of the nobleman, a station in life open to all who seek it. After all, it is a poor democracy that cannot afford a little aristocracy, especially the aristocracy of a searching and generous intellect.

mortimer j. adler

Labor, Leisure, and
Liberal Education *

LET ME BEGIN WHERE ANYONE HAS TO BEGIN—WITH A TENTA-tive definition of education. Education is a practical activity. It is concerned with means to be employed or devised for the achievement of an end. The broadest definition with which no one, I think, can disagree is that education is a process which aims at the improvement or betterment of men, in themselves and in relation to society. Few will quarrel with this definition because most people are willing to say that education is good; and its being good requires it to do something that is good for men. The definition says precisely this: that education improves men or makes them better.

All the quarrels that exist in educational philosophy exist because men have different conceptions of what the good life is, of what is good for man, of the conditions under which man is improved or bettered. Within that large area of controversy about education, there is one fundamental distinction that I should like to call to your attention.

There seem to be two ways in which men can be bettered or improved: first, with respect to special functions or talents and, second, with respect to the capacities and functions which are common to all men. Let me explain. In civilized societies, and even in primitive societies, there is always a rudimentary, and often a very complex, division of labor. Society exists through a diversity of occupations, through different groups of men performing different functions. In addition to the division of labor and the consequent diversity of functions, there is the simple natural fact of individual differences. So one view of education is that which takes these individual and functional *differences* into consideration and says that men are made better by adjusting them to their occupations, by making them better carpenters or better dentists or better bricklayers, by improving them, in other words, in the direction of their own special talents.

The other view differs from this in that it makes the primary aim of education the betterment of men not with respect to

* From *Journal of General Education* (Vol. 6, No. 1, October, 1951). By permission of Mortimer J. Adler and the University of Chicago Press.

their differences but with respect to the *similarities* which all men have. According to this theory, if there are certain things that all men *can* do, or certain things that all men *must* do, it is with these that education is chiefly concerned.

This simple distinction leads us to differentiate between specialized education and general education. There is some ground for identifying specialized education with vocational education, largely because specialization has some reference to the division of labor and the diversity of occupations, and for identifying general education with liberal education because the efforts of general education are directed toward the liberal training of man as *man*.

There is still another way of differentiating education in terms of its ends. . . . An educational process has an *intrinsic* end if its result lies entirely within the *person* being educated, an excellence or perfection of his person, an improvement built right into his nature as a good habit is part of the nature of the person in whom a power is habituated. An *extrinsic* end of education, on the other hand, lies in the goodness of an *operation*, not as reflecting the goodness of the operator but rather the perfection of something else as a result of the operation being performed well.

Thus, for example, there can be two reasons for learning carpentry. One might wish to learn carpentry simply to acquire the skill or art of using tools to fabricate things out of wood, an art or skill that anyone is better for having. Or one might wish to learn carpentry in order to make good tables and chairs, not as works of art which reflect the excellence of the artist, but as commodities to sell. This distinction between the two reasons for learning carpentry is connected in my mind with the difference or distinction between liberal and vocational education. This carpentry is the same in both cases, but the first reason for learning carpentry is liberal, the second vocational.

All of this, I think, leads directly to the heart of the matter: that vocational training is training for work or labor; it is specialized rather than general; it is for an extrinsic end; and ultimately it is the education of slaves or workers. And from my point of view it makes no difference whether you say slaves or workers, for you mean that the worker is a man who does nothing but work—a state of affairs which has obtained, by the way, during the whole industrial period, from its beginning *almost* to our day.

Liberal education is education for leisure; it is general in character; it is for an intrinsic and not an extrinsic end; and, as compared with vocational training, which is the education of slaves or workers, liberal education is the education of free men.

I would like, however, to add one basic qualification at this point. According to this definition or conception of liberal education, it is not restricted in any way to training in the liberal arts. We often too narrowly identify liberal education with those arts which are genuinely the liberal arts—grammar, rhetoric and logic and the mathematical disciplines—because that is one of the traditional meanings of liberal education. But, as I am using the term "liberal" here, in contradistinction to "vocational," I am not confining liberal education to intellectual education or to the cultivation of the mind. On the contrary, as I am using the phrase, liberal education has three large departments, according to the division of human excellences or modes of perfection. Physical training or gymnastics in the Platonic sense, if its aim is to produce a good co-ordination of the body, is liberal education. So also is moral training, if its aim is to produce moral perfections, good moral habits or virtues; and so also is intellectual training, if its aim is the production of good intellectual habits or virtues. All three are liberal as distinguished from vocational. This is not, in a sense, a deviation from the conception of liberal education as being concerned only with the mind, for in all three of these the mind plays a role. All bodily skills are arts; all moral habits involve prudence; so the mind is not left out of the picture even when one is talking about moral and physical training.

After this purely preliminary statement, I should like to spend most of the remaining time on the problem of what labor is, and what leisure is, and how these two things are related. For as understanding of these two terms becomes clearer, I think understanding of liberal education and of the problem of liberal education in our society will become clearer.

Let me begin by considering the parts of a human life—and by "the parts of a human life" I mean the division of the twenty-four hours of each day in the succession of days that make up the weeks, months, and years of our lives. The lives of all of us today are divided roughly into thirds. This was not always the case. The lives of the slaves of antiquity and, until recently, the wage-slaves of our modern industrial society were divided into two parts, not three. We are, however, accustomed to think of our lives as having three parts.

One-third is sleep. I include with sleep—because they belong to the same category, and I shall use "sleep" as a symbol of all such things—*eating* (in so far as it is not liberal, in so far as it is quite apart from conversation, eating just to sustain the body); the acts of *washing* and *cleansing* the body; and even *exercise,* in so far as it is indispensable for physical fitness. These things are like sleep because they maintain the body as a biological mechanism.

Sleep, then, is one-third; work or labor, one-third; and one-third is free time or spare time. I am defining the latter negatively now, as time not spent in sleep or work, time free from work or biological necessities. Now I say this threefold division of the parts of a day (and, therefore, a human life) into sleep and the adjuncts of sleep, work or labor, and free or spare time is not entirely satisfactory. A further division is required. Free time, it is clear, may be used in two ways when it is not used, as some people use it, for sleep and other biological necessities. One of the two ways in which free time can be used is play—and by "play" I mean recreation, amusement, diversion, pastime, and, roughly, all ways of killing time. The other use of free or spare time I should like to denominate roughly for the moment—I will analyze it more carefully later—engagement in leisure activities. If you say, "What do you mean by leisure activities?" I answer, "Such things as thinking or learning, reading or writing, conversation or correspondence, love and acts of friendship, political activity, domestic activity, artistic and aesthetic activity." Just think of that list of things. They are not work, and they are not, or they seem not to be, play. Here is a group of activities which occupy time free from sleep and work and which are distinct from recreation or amusement. But the line of distinction is not clear, nor is the definition of the class of activities. . . .

Let me see if I can explain the differences of work, play and leisure activity. Certain criteria, which are often used to distinguish work, play and leisure, fail, I think, to define these three things. For example, persons often use the criterion of pleasure and pain, somehow thinking of work as painful and play or leisure as pleasant. It is immediately apparent, I think, that this is incorrect. Play can be quite painful. What does one mean by speaking of a "grueling" match of tennis, if one does not mean that there is often physical pain in playing a long, fast tennis match? Work certainly can be pleasant. There is actual pleasure in a skilled performance, even if the performance is part of a laborious activity. And leisure activities, if I am right in thinking that learning is a typical leisure activity, certainly can be quite painful. Note, moreover, a very common phrase, one used in school, namely, *school work* or *home work*. Though school work and home work are study and are therefore a part of learning and belong to leisure activity, we call them "work." Why? Because there is some pain involved? I think not. I think we call them "work," as I shall try to show you subsequently, not because pain is involved in them but because we do them under some obligation, under some compulsion. This is the first indication that the meaning of "work" somehow involves the compulsory.

Fatigue is a second criterion that is often used to distinguish work, play or leisure. All forms of activity can be tiring, and all forms of activity which involve both the mind and the body call for sleep to wash away fatigue. Nor is it true to say that work is difficult and play and leisure are easy, for play and leisure activities can be difficult, too. Nor do I think that the Thomistic division of the good into the useful, the pleasant and the virtuous will by itself (although I think it comes near to it) perfectly distinguish between work as the useful, play as the pleasant and leisure as the virtuous. Unless those terms are more sharply restricted, I think one could regard work as pleasant or even virtuous in a sense; play as useful in so far as it is recreative and performs a biological function; and leisure activities, although they may be intrinsically virtuous, as useful and pleasant. Let me therefore offer a criterion which I think will succeed in drawing the line between labor and leisure and will take care of play as well.

Though it may not perfectly account for play, I would like to propose that the distinction between labor or work, on the one hand, and leisure activities, on the other, is to be made in terms of what is biologically necessary or compulsory and what is rationally or humanly desirable or free. Let me see if I can explain this criterion by applying it. Labor, I say, is an economically necessary activity. It is something you do to produce the means of subsistence. It makes no difference at all whether the worker gets consumable goods immediately by his laboring activity or wages wherewith to buy consumable goods. Let us think of this for a moment in the following way. Let consumable goods—either direct consumables or money—be the compensation of the laborer; and, further, let us assume for the moment that no man gets his subsistence in the form of either consumable goods or money without labor. Then the definition of work or labor is: that activity which is required, is compulsory, for all men in order for them to live or subsist and which therefore must be extrinsically compensated, that is, the laborer must earn by his labor the means of his subsistence.

Let us test this. Men who have ample and secure means of subsistence have no need to labor. This is the historical meaning of the leisure class. Provide any man or group of men with ample and secure means of subsistence, and they will not work. I do not mean that they will not be active, that they will not be productive, that they will not be creative, but they will not work. They will not labor in the sense in which I tried to define that term sharply. Anything they will do will have to have for them some *intrinsic compensation*. Strictly, the word "compensation" is here wrongly used. The activities in which they engage will have to be *intrinsically rewarding*. What they do will somehow be done for its own sake, since they are provided with the means of subsistence. . . .

Leisure activities, in sharp distinction from labor or work, consist of those things that men do because they are desirable for their own sake. They are self-rewarding, not externally compensated, and they are freely engaged in. They may be morally necessary, but they are not biologically compulsory. You can see the trouble with this definition as soon as you say it. You may ask at once, "What is play? Is not play self-rewarding? Is not play distinguished from labor by the negative distinction that it is something you do not have to do? Something that you freely choose to do?"

I think we can get some light on how to sharpen the definition of leisure, and keep it distinct from play, by etymological considerations. I must confess to being genuinely fascinated by the background of the word "leisure." The word which in Greek means "leisure" is *scole*. Notice that our English word "school" comes from *scole*.

Now the Greek word *scole* has two meanings, just as the English word "pastime" has two meanings. In the dictionary the first meaning of "pastime" refers to the time itself, to *spare* time. The second meaning of "pastime" refers to what is done with such time, namely, *play*. It is this second meaning that we usually intend by our use of the word. So the first meaning of *scole* refers to the time; the second to the content or use of the time. The first is leisure in the merely negative sense of time *free from* labor, or spare time; but the second meaning, which appears very early in Greek literature, refers to what men should *do* with this time, namely, learn and discuss. It is the second meaning—what one does with time free from labor —which permits *scole* to become the root of the word "school." This, it seems to me, throws a fascinating light on a phrase that was used frequently in my youth when boys of sixteen faced, with their parents, the question, "Shall I go to *work* or shall I go to *school?*" Making this a choice of opposites is quite right, because work is one thing and school is another. *It is the difference between labor and leisure.*

When we look for the Latin equivalent of the Greek word *scole*, more light is thrown on the subject. The first meaning, time free from work or labor, appears in the Latin word *otium*. *Otium* is the root of the word *negotium*, which means "negotiation" or "business." *Otium* is the very opposite of *negotium* or "business"; it simply means time *free from* work. What is wonderful here is that the English word "otiose" is not a very complimentary word—it means "unemployed, idle, sterile, futile, useless." The second meaning of *scole* is translated by the Latin *schola*. This again is a source of "school." Finally, the first meaning of *otium* has a synonym in Latin, *vacatio*, from which we get the word "vacation" and also, interestingly enough, "vacancy."

The English word "leisure" comes down a totally different line. It comes from the French *loisir*, and from the Latin *licere*; it has the root meaning of the permissible and the free. The Latin *licere* is also the root of "liberty" and "license," in addition to "leisure." I think it is extraordinary to see these three words related in that one Latin root.

In the light of this etymology, I think we can distinguish leisure from play as two quite different uses of free or spare time, that is, *not working time*. Play may be one of two things. It may be biologically useful like sleep, just as vacations and recreational activities are biologically useful. Just as sleep is a way of washing away fatigue, so a certain amount of play or vacation or recreation has the same kind of biological utility in the recuperation of the body. Play may be, however, something in excess of this. Obviously, children play to excess; they do not play just to refresh themselves. And I often wonder whether this does not have a bearing on the role of play in adult life, that is, whether or not the role of play in adult life is not always a temporary regression to childhood. I ask this question quite seriously, because after one has passed the point where play is biologically useful, all it can be is otiose, sterile and useless.

One can admit, I think, that life involves two kinds of play; play for the sake of work, when it serves the same purpose as sleep, and play for its own sake. Sensual pleasure is admittedly a part of human life, but only in a limited quantity. Beyond that you have licentiousness; so, too, licentious play is a misuse of leisure.

Certainly, no quality attaches to useless play other than pleasure. I, for one, can see no perfection, no improvement, resulting from it. But leisure consists of those intrinsically good activities which are both self-rewarding and meaningful beyond themselves. They need not be confined to themselves. They can be both good things to do and good in their results, as, for example, political activities, the activities of a citizen, are both good in themselves and good in their results. This does not mean that leisure activities are never terminal, never without ends *beyond* themselves; it means only that they must be good *in themselves,* things worth doing even if there were no need for them to be done.

The results of leisure activity are two sorts of human excellence or perfection: those private excellences by which a man perfects his own nature and those public excellences which can be translated into the performance of his moral or political duty—the excellence of a man in relation to other men and to society. Hence I would define leisure activities as those activities desirable for their own sake (and so uncompensated and not compulsory) and also for the sake of the excellences, private and public, to which they give rise. This means, by the way, that *leisure activities are identical with virtue.* . . .

Suppose we draw a line between economically or biologically useful activities and those which are morally or humanly good. . . . What results from making this separation? We get a threefold division: from the biologically necessary, we get sleep, work and play (in so far as these serve to recuperate the body or to remove fatigue); from the humanly, morally good, the noble or honorable, we get all leisure activities; and from the superfluous, the otiose, we again get play, but here we mean play as it consists entirely in killing or wasting time, however pleasant that may be.

We see, furthermore, that the very same activities can be either labor or leisure, according to the conditions under which they are performed. Let us take manual work again—for instance, carpentry. Manual work can be leisure if it is work done for the sake of the art that is involved and for the cultivation of an artist. It is labor if it is done for compensation. That example may be too obvious, but we can see the same thing in teaching or painting, composing music, or political action of any sort. Any one of these can be labor as well as leisure, if a person does it in order to earn his subsistence. For if, to begin with, one accepts the proposition that no man shall get food or clothing or shelter, no man shall get the means of subsistence, without earning them, then some activities which would otherwise be leisure must be done by some persons for compensation. This makes them no less intrinsically rewarding but gives them an additional character. This double character causes certain activities to be labor, looked at one way, and leisure, looked at another.

This accounts for the fact that in professors' lives or statesmen's lives the line between labor and leisure is almost impossible to draw. . . .

Not only can the same activity be both leisure and work; but even play, or things that I would call play, can be work for some people. Professional football is work to those who play it. Think also of all the persons whose working lives are spent in the amusement business.

This leads to further interesting points about the kinds of work. . . . Taking both manual and mental work into consideration together, I would like to make the distinction between productive and nonproductive labor. I would say that work or labor is productive when it is economically useful, that is, when it produces means of subsistence in one form or another.

Here it is proper for the mode of compensation to consist of wages (or, as they are called more politely, "salaries"), with some basis for what we call a fair wage in a relation of equivalence between the amount of labor and the product of labor. Nonproductive labors, on the other hand, are activities which may be called work only in the sense that they are compensated —such things as teaching, artistic creation, the professional work of medicine and law, and the activities of statesmen. Here it is wrong to use the words "wages" or "salary"; and it is interesting to note that the language contains other words. We speak of an "honorarium" or "fee"; but the word I like best is the word "living" in the sense in which a priest gets not wages or a salary but a *living*. He is *given* his subsistence. He has not earned it by *production*. He has done something which it is good to do, but he also has to live; and there is a sense in which he can be said to have "earned his living." Here there can be no calculation of fair compensation. When one talks about fees or honoraria, the only thing one can talk about is the amount of time spent. Lawyers very often set their fees entirely in terms of time.

I would like to make a second distinction—between servile and liberal work. I think it is difficult to draw the line between these two, except in extreme cases, because many kinds of labor or work are *partly servile* and *partly liberal*. But the extreme cases are quite clear; and it is important at least to recognize the mixed cases or the shadowy ones that lie between.

By "servile work" I mean work done only because it is economically necessary and done only for compensation—work that no one would do if the means of subsistence were otherwise provided. "Liberal work" is work or activity which, though sometimes done for compensation, would be done even if no compensation were involved, because the work itself is self-rewarding. In other words, liberal work contains, at its very heart, activities that are essentially leisure activities, things that would be done for their own sake, even though subsistence were otherwise secured. The consequence of this is that the man who is a liberal worker—a teacher, lawyer, statesman or creative artist—may, and usually does, work many more hours than are required for his compensation. He does more than is necessary to do a fair job for the person who is compensating him, because he cannot determine the point at which his activity passes into strictly leisure activity. In fact, it would be more accurate to say that all his time is spent in leisure activity, though some part of it earns his compensation. I think examples of the research scientist, the teacher or the statesman make this perfectly clear.

Finally, in terms of these distinctions, there is at least the beginning of an order for the parts of life. It would seem to me that, by the very nature of the terms themselves, sleep and its adjunct activities and play as recreation must be for the sake of work; and work must be for the sake of leisure. Earning a living, in short, and keeping alive must be for the sake of living well. Many of the obvious disorders of human life result from improper understanding of the order of these parts—for example, sleeping for its own sake, which is at least neurotic and at worst suicidal; working as an end in itself, which is a complete perversion of human life; working for the sake of play, which is certainly a misconception of leisure; or free time as time to kill in pleasure-seeking. Play for its own sake, in order to kill time or escape boredom, is as neurotic as sleep for its own sake. . . .

In terms of this very brief and sketchy analysis of the parts of life, and of these fairly difficult distinctions between work, play and leisure activities, we now can see clearly the difference between vocational training and liberal education. Vocational training is learning for the sake of earning. I hope I step on nobody's toes too hard when I say, as I must say, that therefore it is an absolute misuse of school to include any vocational training at all. School is a place of learning for the sake of learning, not for the sake of earning. It is as simple as that. Please understand that I do not mean vocational training can be totally dispensed with; I mean only that it should be done on the job. It should be done as preparatory to work; and as preparatory to work, it should be compensated. No one should have to take vocational training without compensation, because it is not self-rewarding. To include vocational training in school *without compensation* is to suppose that it is education, which it is not at all. In contrast to vocational training, liberal education is learning for its own sake or for the sake of further education. It is learning for the sake of all those self-rewarding activities which include the political, aesthetic and speculative.

There are three further comments I should like to make on this distinction. First, professional education can be both vocational and liberal, because the kind of work for which it is the preliminary training is essentially liberal work. The work of a lawyer is liberal, not servile, work. In Greece free men who were citizens were all lawyers; there education for legal practice was liberal education. Professional education is vocational only in so far as this kind of leisure activity happens to be a way that some men, in our division of labor, earn their compensation.

Second, liberal education can involve work simply because we find it necessary to compel children to begin, and for some years to continue, their educations. Whenever you find an adult, a chronological adult, who thinks that learning or study is work, let me say that you have met a child. One sign that you are grown up, that you are no longer a child, is that you never regard any part of study or learning as work. As long as learning or study has anything compulsory about it, you are still in the condition of childhood. The mark of truly adult learning is that it is done with no thought of labor or work at all, with no sense of the compulsory. It is entirely voluntary. Liberal education at the adult level can, therefore, be superior to liberal education in school, where learning is identified with work.

Third, if schooling is equivalent to the proper use of leisure time in youth, then the proper use of leisure time in adult life should obviously include the continuation of schooling—without teachers, without compulsion, without assignments—the kind of learning that adults do outside school, the kind they do in conversations and discussions, in reading and study.

Finally, we may ask the place of liberal education in an industrial democracy. We can do this quickly by considering two basic errors or fallacies peculiar to our society; the first I would call the aristocratic error; the second, the industrial fallacy.

The aristocratic error is simply the error of dividing men into free men and slaves or workers, into a leisure class and a working class, instead of dividing the time of each human life into working time and leisure time. In the last few weeks I have been reading Karl Marx's *Das Kapital* and, quite apart from the theory of surplus value—Marx's special notion of capitalistic production—the book, as you know, is filled with the horrible facts about the life of the laboring classes until almost our own day. We must face the fact that, until very recently, the working classes did nothing but *sleep and work*. When we realize that children started to work at the age of seven; that whole families worked—men, women and children; that the hours of working time were often twelve and fourteen hours a day, sometimes seven days a week, then we realize that the distinction between the leisure class and the working class is something you and I no longer can appreciate because it has disappeared from our society. It does not exist in the world today, at least not in the United States. But, if we consider the past, in which workers were like slaves, the aristocratic error consisted in the division of mankind into two classes, a leisure class and a working class.

To correct this error, we must say not only that all men are free but also that all men must work for their subsistence (which is nothing but a democratic or socialist variant on the biblical admonition that man must eat by the sweat of his brow). You will see the educational consequences of this fallacy when you stop to think how little point there would have been in talking about liberal education for all men in the eighteenth and nineteenth centuries, when much more than half the population had no time for education. It would have been just as meaningless for them to have been given a liberal education, doomed as they were to lead lives of work and sleep.

The second fallacy arises from the fact that industrial production has created an abundance of leisure time for all. I do not mean that the working classes today have as much leisure time as the leisure classes of other centuries. I mean simply that more leisure exists today, per capita, than ever existed before. Though industrial production has produced this abundance of leisure, industrialism as such has made all men servants of productivity; and, when productivity itself is regarded as the highest good, leisure is debased to the level of play or idleness, which can be justified only as recreation. The man of leisure is regarded by industrialists, interested solely in productivity, as either a playboy or a dilettante. Leisure loses its meaning when industrial society reduces it to an incidental by-product of productivity.

If these two fallacies are corrected, we reach, I think, the obvious conclusion that in a rightly conceived industrial democracy, liberal education *should be* and *can be* for all men. It should be because they are all equal as persons, as citizens, from a democratic point of view. It can be because industrialism can emancipate all men from slavery and because workers in our day need not spend their entire lives earning their livings. Liberal education in the future of democracy should be and should do for all men what it once was and did for the few in the aristocracies of the past. It should be part of the lives of all men.

But I may be asked whether I have forgotten about individual differences. Even if all men are citizens, even if they are emancipated from the complete drudgery of labor, it still is not true that all men are equally endowed with talent or have an equal capacity to lead the good life. . . .

The good or happy life is a life lived in the cultivation of virtue. Another way of saying this is that the good life or the happy life is concerned with leisure. The good life *depends on labor,* but it *consists of leisure.* Labor and all conditions that go with labor are the antecedent means of happiness. They are external goods, that is, *wealth.* Leisure activities are the ends for which wealth is the means. Leisure activities are the constituents of happiness. Leisure activities constitute not mere living but living well.

Happiness so conceived is open to all men, *when all men are both workers and free men.* As regards both work and leisure, each man should do the best work and participate in the best sort of leisure activities of which he is capable, the highest for which his talents equip him. So conceived, happiness is the same for all men, though it differs in actual content, in degree of intensity, according to the individual differences of men.

It is clear, I think, that liberal education is absolutely necessary for human happiness, for living a good human life. The most prevalent of all human ills are these two: a man's discontent with the work he does and the necessity of having to kill time. Both these ills can be, in part, cured by liberal education. Liberal schooling prepares for a life of learning and for the leisure activities of a whole lifetime. Adult liberal education is an indispensable part of the life of leisure, which is a life of learning.

j. roby kidd

Liberal Education for Business Leadership *

MY SUBJECT CAN BE EASILY STATED. IF THE PROPER STUDY OF mankind is man, the proper topic for an educational or training program is how to bring out the potentialities that lie within men and women. In particular, *what kind of education or training is required to unlock those human qualities that are needed in guiding great modern businesses?*

I realize it is presumptuous of me to fumble with a question that has attracted the wisest and noblest spirits of all ages. But surely, inasmuch as this question is of such consequence, it should stir us to consider together what it means for us, not simply accept what others have said about it.

Today there is dread felt by millions of men and women about what the machine may do to them. . . . They can be told that when muscle power is replaced by machine power the result will be an enriched opportunity for all their human qualities. But we must not underestimate their misgivings that somehow in the process they may become demeaned and dwarfed, serfs to a machine or an economic process.

And yet, if we think about it, it is quite apparent that in

* From *Adult Leadership* (May, 1957). By permission of the Adult Education Association of the U. S. A.

this age of science and the Univac, it is human qualities that will count most. . . .

Recently the president of one of Canada's strongest companies told me of his dilemma. He has fifty younger executives. Each one of them is well qualified in such fields as engineering, sales, accounting and advertising. But, he claims, not one of them is ready to succeed him.

I asked him why. First of all, he said, none of them knows enough about public affairs, or national and international issues. But that is not too serious because they can all learn. More difficult is that none of them has a framework or a scheme of values against which to cast and evaluate the needed knowledge. Last, and worst of all, none of them seems to realize that he lacks anything.

Now I do not know if that president was being fair to his associates, and I have no way of knowing if this judgment would apply to other industries. Still, it does sharpen up what we are talking about.

Clarence Francis, retired president of General Foods Corporation, once said, "You can buy a man's time, you can buy a man's physical presence at a given place, you can even buy a measured number of skilled muscular actions per hour or day. But you cannot buy enthusiasm, you cannot buy initiative, you cannot buy loyalty, you cannot buy the devotion of heart, mind, and soul. You have to earn these things."

Is there any kind of education which will equip business leaders to cope with such responsibilities?

For centuries claims have been made that education, at least a certain kind of education, does have such results. It is an education that seeks for meanings, is concerned about relationships and values, formulates principles and solves problems. It is usually called liberal education, or the liberal arts, or the humanities.

I am not suggesting that there are no distinctions between these terms, but they are often used loosely as synonyms to describe a particular kind of education, the kind that Sir Arthur Currie, president of McGill University, was speaking about when he said, "The primary task of education is to make men alive, to send them out alive at more points, alive on higher levels, alive in more effective ways. The purpose of an education is not the mere getting of the ability to sell your efforts at a higher figure than unlearned men do, but to make you a thinker, to make you a creator, with an enlarged capacity for life."

Let us consider this claim. Does it imply that there is no place for vocational or technical education? Of course not. I believe it was A. L. Nickerson, of the Socony-Mobil Oil Company, who said, "We know that when we are looking for men with executive ability to promote, their technical knowledge at that stage is often relatively less important than their ability to deal with more abstract problems involving judgment and ability to reason. There is, in fact, a sort of crossing of lines in this regard. While a man's technical knowledge may be his best tool during his first five years or so with our company, in many cases this curve tends to flatten out on the value chart and is met by the ascendant curve of the man's skill in human relations and other factors. . . ."

I have stated that the view about the primary place of the liberal arts for training mind and character has been held throughout the ages. But, in surprising measure, it has been advanced by business executives during the past five or ten years, and not just in talk either. Standard Oil, Ford, General Foods, General Electric, Bethlehem Steel, Procter & Gamble and Du Pont (and I could go on and on with the list) are making a substantial cash contribution to liberal studies in the universities in addition to support afforded scientific and medical research. . . .

In fact, so much has been said about the values of liberal education by businessmen that zealots for the liberal arts, by their extravagance, seem to have stirred up opponents who have had little difficulty demonstrating that odd bits and pieces of the classics, a kind of cultural cocktail made up of a dram of Plato, a dash of Kant and a squirt of Beethoven, are not much good for anybody, let alone a busy executive. . . .

With all respect, it seems to me that we have spent too much time on the wrong question. Instead of debating whether a liberal education provides the best training for top management we ought to be putting it in concrete and more modest terms. Under what conditions or arrangements can the liberal arts prepare executives for leadership?

I should like to state, very tentatively, some of the conditions which I believe are necessary if we are to have the kind of liberal or *liberating* education we recognize as being necessary.

Alfred P. Sloan has often declared, "Give us *educated* men. We can *train* them ourselves. But we cannot *educate* them." But, as Mr. Sloan understands very well, the kind of education he refers to is initiated, but not completed, in college halls. Much of what constitutes a genuine liberal education is just not possible for a youngster. He can read about it and consider the problems intellectually. But the real significance of much of ethics, philosophy and drama can only come to a man well past his youth whose deepening experiences of family, vocation and community enable him to see and feel and understand new relationships and begin to judge values.

This point is elementary and obvious enough. But we have been rather slow in its application. Learning may and does go on all through life, but *education* denoting some plan or shaping or purpose of learning only happens if there is provision for it. How well equipped are our libraries, universities, trade associations and voluntary organizations for continuous education? . . .

In the years since the war the number of opportunities for mature men and women to carry on systematic liberal studies has increased at an accelerating rate. Some corporations and universities which have a far-sighted plan for the training of executives have acquired estates or camps so that such programs can be conducted in residence. We are beginning to understand the values of residential education, where men share a variety of experiences with enough isolation and leisure to explore meanings and relationships. This was once the privilege of a comparative handful of undergraduates; now it is available to increasing numbers of men and women. This is a promising start, but only a start.

Liberal education was once the prerogative of an aristocracy. It is not surprising, then, that it is still regarded as something for a special few, a tiny elite of towering intellect and sensibility. Cynics also share this view and some of them speak derisively of a tiny minority of *eggheads* and *longhairs* standing coldly aside from the great masses of people. It is part of the same myth that the multitude of normal folk are supposed to care for nothing, or respond to nothing, but football games and giveaway programs.

This is a pernicious falsehood. Of course, there are wide differences in people, and in their capacity and their ability to take part in certain activities. Moreover, if a man has never had any experience of the power of drama, or the beauty of music, or the excitement possible in the clash of ideas, it is little wonder that he would not choose to spend time in these ways.

But once he does participate *with satisfaction*, he is never quite the same person. Those who have talked with the humblest farmers or mechanics in colonial territories about what will happen with the advent of self-determination and self-government have observed the quickening that comes to any man who is gripped with a large idea.

Then there is the Shakespearean Festival held each summer at Stratford, Canada. Was it a university that started this great arts festival? No. What about the *elite* who planned and managed it? A chemist, a newspaper reporter, a factory manager, a druggist, an engineer, a salesman, an accountant, two housewives and a Baptist minister comprised the elite. And who, do you suppose, fill up the seats in the tent auditorium night after night to witness the plays of Shakespeare and Sophocles? Well, Brooks Atkinson and other critics come for opening night. But the rest of the season it is stenographers and office workers, truck drivers and shopkeepers, plumbers and farmers, teachers and students. These people stand patiently in queues for seats and, after each performance, stumble out into the night shaken and stirred and bewildered and exhilarated by the majesty and dread of great drama.

Does liberal education leave out science? Why should it? The history of science, the scientific attitude or scientific ethic must, I would think, be an important part of any liberal curriculum. So should the philosophical and ethical problems of modern business organization. Would you think, for example, that a man was liberally educated who had not pondered deeply over such an idea as "What's good for General Motors is good for the country?"

Surely there are two misleading assumptions, as a thoughtful university head in England recently pointed out, that must be guarded against. The first is that the classics are necessarily of supreme value. "No one," said Eric Ashby, "denies that classical humanism deals with the perennially important issues: goodness and evil, beauty and ugliness, justice, truth; but there is plenty of evidence that it no longer reaches the bloodstream of society; and if it does not, it is impotent." Ashby also denies the second assumption, that technology itself cannot embrace the humanities. "Humanism is concerned with the creative arts of man; these include airplanes as well as Gothic churches, and textiles as well as poetry."

Liberal or liberating education is often confounded with classical education. About once a year I hear a speech by someone who claims that the only basis for a genuine education is Latin, Greek and Philosophy. Somehow, I have the feeling that no one would oppose such a boast so strenuously as would Aristotle or Thomas Aquinas if they were around today. Such a view, it seems to me, is a profound denial and betrayal of all that is wisest and best in the great humane classical tradition. It is not simply by studying the words or works of great men in the past that our spirits will be quickened, our minds stretched and our tastes purified. The curriculum would hardly fail to seek health and life from the great spirits of the past—increasingly, I believe, from men of the Orient as well as of the West. But it is not antiquity that is important, but the breadth and depth and intensity of the experience; where it leads to, not its point of origin.

No adult ought to put up with shabby, threadbare lectures. A liberal education means to open up the mind, not seal it tight with drab formulas or a "closed-circuit system" of ideas. The adult student ought to participate, to try out ideas, to test hypotheses, to judge and dissent. There is no code of truth to be memorized; there are experiences to be tasted and tested.

Some of the teaching methods worked out in courses of business administration ought to have just as much validity in the liberal arts. My field of teaching is not philosophy, but if it were I am sure I would frequently employ the *case method*. One can almost picture Socrates, with a glint in his eye, plunging into the consideration of ethics and morals as exhibited in an *incident* or *case*.

No truly liberating education can be limited to verbal or mathematical symbols. We ought to recall one judgment from the *Harvard Report:* "Precisely because they wear the warmth and color of the senses, the arts are probably the strongest and deepest of all educative forces." Emotions are of vital importance.

I have a suspicion that all of us may assent to this, perhaps even quote it on some pertinent occasions, but do little or nothing about its implications.

It is true that industry is giving encouragement to the arts. And they have done so on the only basis that the artist finds acceptable—by bringing the artist in as a co-worker to create things of beauty and utility for the company.

Despite this fact I have the feeling that many of us are still a little distrustful of those things that call forth a deep emotional response, as if there was something a little shameful about it. Many of us boast about our fishing or golf prowess but might be rather careful to whom we would confide the information that we had spent a weekend sketching or singing with a choral group. However, we ought to be grateful for gains in this respect in recent years.

Like you, I have had men ask me, "Will a particular course produce better salesmen?" I have had to reply that I did not know and that there could be no assurance that it would. Men who will seriously take part in a course of liberal studies will probably be more alert, more thoughtful and more sensitive to people and things around them. In the long run, I believe this is good for business. But the mere reading of Plato's *Republic* will not push up anyone's sales graph. We need to be honest, and modest, about educational accomplishments.

I come now to a condition which is not easy to state although I am convinced of its validity. Let me put it bluntly.

The liberal studies have little power for good unless you are ready to accept them on their own terms. One cannot make of them a gimmick, a trick or a device. It is rather like the old fables where the magic would only work for those who had faith. In the same way, the liberal studies have power only when approached by the pure in heart. I mean by those who seek them for their intrinsic ends, judgments, values, understanding—and not as a talisman or union card necessary for executive promotion.

In the past twenty-five years many laudable attempts have been made to simplify, condense, or make material more interesting or readable. One result is that pamphlets and annual reports are, on the whole, vastly improved. But some ideas are not simple and they cannot be comprehended without effort. Attempts to primerize always seem to be condescending, to talk down, and to present half-truths and distortions.

Recently a booklet arrived from England with a warning printed on the cover. It read: "There is nothing in this booklet which most men and women cannot understand. But the subject is sufficiently difficult that you will be obliged to read carefully and thoughtfully. If you are not prepared to do this there is little point in your going further."

Surprising or not this approach seems to have achieved an excellent response. Most people can and will give attention if they believe that the effort is worth while. They have no patience with needless obscurity, but they do not want to be babied either. They are able to brook more complexity than is characterized by the early television movies (alas still with us) when every hero was shown astride a *white* horse while all the "bad guys" are riding on brown or black horses.

There is a cost to this? Of course. You would rightly question it, and be suspicious, if there were none.

The first cost is dollars.

The second cost is imagination.

The third cost is hospitality to differences. We must remember that the products of a genuinely liberal education will not all look, or talk, or think alike. If you give human beings a chance to grow you can never predict the outcome. If men are deeply stirred they will respond in ways that may seem wonderful, curious, alarming or grotesque.

Of course, if we hate or fear difference, if we cannot brook dissent, if we are certain that all the right answers are already known, then let us eschew liberal education for the enemy it is. But perhaps we ought to remind ourselves that the qualities of many, perhaps most, of the men who have most influenced our era were not readily identified.

A former president of the Rockefeller Foundation used to ask himself regularly once a week if he would have seen the potential promise and would have been willing to support the young Pasteur when he was struggling away in his early garret laboratory. Being certain about other kinds of excellence in the early crude stages is even more difficult. But if we can bear to work alongside a man who does or says or thinks unusual things, if we can tolerate or even relish association with those who question some of our assumptions, all of us may learn something.

peter f. drucker

Social Innovation *

AMONG THE MAJOR INNOVATIONS OF THE PAST TEN OR FIFTEEN years, only one can even remotely be called an innovation in product or productive process. That is the development of systematic and organized methods of materials handling. Otherwise, in their aggregate, the basically nontechnological innovations have had a greater impact on the American economy, and have contributed more to the increase in productivity in this country, than all technological innovations of the past ten or fifteen years. In the long view of history, it is for social inventions—and not technical ones—that Americans may be best remembered.

During the period ahead, in any event, the greatest need for innovation seems more likely to lie in the social than in the technological area. Indeed, the technological revolution itself will be totally unproductive unless it is accompanied by major innovations in the nontechnological field. Among them, above all, is again innovation in marketing. Equally badly needed are innovations in methods, tools and measurements for doing the managerial job in the modern enterprise, large or small; for the development of competence, skill and imagination among managers (still considered a luxury by many companies) is probably the greatest necessity any business, let alone the economy, faces. Finally, the need is for effective innovation in the management of workers and in the organization of work; despite the progress in this area, it may well be the most backward sphere, and the one with the greatest potential for increased productivity.

* From *America's Next Twenty Years* (New York, Harper & Brothers, 1957). By permission of Peter F. Drucker and Harper & Brothers.

Compared to electronics, rocket engines or synthetic chemistry, these are unglamorous subjects. They are rarely discussed except by professional managers, and not as often as they should be, even so. Yet our success at innovating in these four areas may well decide whether the population revolution, which has already taken place, will be an opportunity for further growth and strength, or whether it will prove a strain, a burden, and perhaps even a threat to social and economic stability.

robert j. blakely

The Free Individual and the Free Society *

ONE EVENING RECENTLY MY CHILDREN DRAGGED OUR DOG—aging, fat, philosophical Radish—into what is humorously called Daddy's study to watch the TV program "Rin-Tin-Tin." They couldn't understand why he did not respond: he had no "felt need" for Rin-Tin-Tin. Later I tried to explain. I began with the paradox that to be is not to be—to be one thing is to not be another. I told what little I know about dog thought —how Radish could not conceive the images. I was about to proceed to human thought, but Susan turned on the radio. "He's Rin-Tin-Tin the fifth," she said. Since I was not able to tell my children about human thought, I am going to tell you.

The movement in modern thought is unmistakably toward relatedness: relating the part and the whole without the neglect of either; relating form and process; relating differences and commonalities; relating thought and emotion, and different kinds of thought such as analytical and intuitive.

Many pieces of driftwood show the current. There are new joint words such as biochemistry, psychosomatic, social psychology. There are new blanket words such as ecology. New meanings are given to old words such as form, pattern, process. There is the attempt to state universal human rights. There is a groping for the idea which will serve for our time the purpose that natural law served in the Middle Ages and the Renaissance.

Because of the nature of modern thought, we must regard developing ideas as provisional and tentative. "This too shall pass away." But each generation must address itself to the

* By permission of Robert J. Blakely and The Fund for Adult Education.

task in hand, and the task of our generations is to relate.

I illustrate with two familiar dualisms of ideas: "matter versus life" and "body versus mind."

Intuitively we have a deep uneasiness about the supposed dualism between matter and life. How many times have we, in reflection, raised up our eyes to the mountains! There we have seen the snows, which, melting, nourish the trees, which bear the fruits, which give us the strength to start a new day. How many times have we, in this thin atmosphere, caught our breath sharply—and then used that breath to utter immortal thoughts!

In *analytical* thought, too, we are becoming increasingly dissatisfied by the dualism between matter and life. One reason—to go no further—is that it must now be recognized that we have no fundamental knowledge of either. Two stories, to illustrate—one about a constituent of matter, the other about the values of life.

A professor of physics asked a student, "What is electricity?" The student puzzled, then replied: "I did know, but I forgot." The professor smote his brow. "My God! The only man who ever knew what electricity is has forgotten!"

In 1939, James Conant, then president of Harvard, was called to Washington to help judge the possibilities of nuclear fission. He told his vice-president that he would be gone a long time, that he could not tell why, and that he could be called only on matters of the highest importance. Weeks passed. One day, during a report on a crucial experiment, a guard whispered to Mr. Conant that his vice-president was calling. Mr. Conant, reflecting that he had not been called previously, concluded that a matter of the highest importance had arisen. During a "break" he returned the call. He heard the voice of the vice-president, trembling with excitement: "Mr. Conant, Harvard has just acquired a Gutenberg Bible!"

We have no fundamental knowledge about either matter or life, but we do know a great deal more about both than we used to know. It is strange indeed to depreciate life rather than exalt it when, through living mind, we make advances in understanding. We don't know how much we *can* or *cannot* understand. But even the awareness of our ignorance can be an instrument in the increase of understanding.

Now, "body versus mind." We are finding out more about how chemicals affect mental states. ("Malt does more than Milton can/ To Justify God's ways to man.") But we are finding out also how mental states affect the internal production of chemicals.

We are probing searchingly into the irrationally conscious, the partially conscious, the subconscious and the unconscious.

So far these insights have been used mainly with regard to sickness. But we are also learning a great deal more about the wellsprings of life that feed the rivers of spontaneity and creativity.

The discovery and exploration of the unconscious and the irrational are achievements of conscious rationality. It is strange indeed that a triumph of the rational should result in a depreciation of the rational. Again, we don't know how much we can or cannot understand, but even the awareness of our ignorance can be an instrument in the increase of understanding.

I will speak now of the individual and society, and then of freedom and responsibility.

I say the individual *and* the society, in relationship, abandoning dualism, although I will be dealing at times with the contrarieties and paradoxes.

There are contrary tendencies in nature. In one direction there is the ceaseless flight of "time's arrow," which cannot return to the bow: entropy, the diffusion of high concentrations of energy to lower and wider distribution; the dissolution of organization to disorganization. The rays which have warmed us this week have been party to the cooling of the sun; the rains which have refreshed us are washing the soil down to the sea; the tumbled rocks which have charmed us are the destruction of the mountains.

In the other direction there is a tendency from disorder toward order, because of instability, imperfection, incompletion. Photons become particles, which become atoms, which become compounds, which make complex formations such as crystals, acids and proteins. With proteins we are on the threshold of life, but we cannot with certainty draw a line to define the point of passing.

Here is the paradox: the sun must shine, the rain must rain, the rocks must disintegrate, in order that life may be and be sustained and evolve; but the forces of dissolution work ceaselessly also on the organization that is life.

The difference between life and nonlife is that life has purpose—its purpose: to live, to grow, to reproduce, to fulfill itself. An example, taken from *The Biology of the Spirit*, by E. W. Sinnott,[1] is the white pine. The branches of a young white pine grow at first straight up, then open and continue upward at about seventy degrees from the trunk. If these branches are tied so that they are held up or down, they will grow for a time as they are compelled, but then they will resume their wonted angle. And we know nothing about the regulatory force which controls this.

[1] Viking Press, 1955.

Living things have purposes. Are not machines also said to have purposes? This is a trick of words. Living things have *their own* purposes. Machines have the "purposes" that men build into them. Whoever heard, asks Joseph Wood Krutch, of an electronic "brain" laughing at itself? I ask further, can you imagine a computer criticizing and evaluating itself?

Are the purposes of living things the design of some greater mind? This we do not know, nor again do we know how much we can or cannot understand. But the awareness of our ignorance chastens analytic thinking and gives scope to intuitive thinking.

An organism has purposes inner to itself. It lives in the "outside"—its environment. To seek its purposes the organism must "know" its environment. The roots of a tree must "know" how to find or make passages between the rocks through which they can seek food and drink. Both organisms and their environment are parts of a larger reality.

Life advances to more complex organization through evolution. Evolution is the process of discovering larger and larger purposes by means of a series of inventions. The human being is an anthology of such inventions—the internal skeleton, the lungs, the circulatory system, the eye, the hand, the brain.

The development is from life which is unconscious, to life which is conscious but not aware of itself, to life which is conscious *and* aware of its consciousness. On a walk yesterday morning I stood and stared a long time at a tree. A tree is alive but it is not conscious. What would it be like to be a tree? (It must be like being in the womb.) Later I stared across a fence at a horse. A horse is alive and conscious but is not aware. What would it be like to be a horse? (It must be like being one year old.) The mature human being is alive and conscious and aware of his consciousness.

Because of this awareness, man has invented a new type of evolution—one which for his purposes frees him from the need for further organic evolution. He can make machines do for him what he would otherwise need radical biological changes to do. If he wants to fly, he does not grow wings: he invents the airplane. If he wants to dive deep in the ocean, he does not revert to gills and change his internal pressures: he invents the submarine. And he can put on and take off these inventions at will—he is not limited by them. For again, to be is not to be—to be something is not to be something else. Man can adopt and slough off the advantages of specialized organic developments while he himself remains unspecialized, unhampered by the disadvantages of wings, gills, overdeveloped muscles or formidable jaw.

We don't know that organic evolution has stopped in man. But we do know that he has reached a plateau upon which for his purposes he needs no more. He holds in his hands and in his mind the direction of his future evolution.

This is a freedom like springing into the air; a responsibility like plunging into the deep. However evolution may work (through randomness, as some think, or through divine plan, as do others), it does not work automatically or sentimentally in the service of man's wants. Certainly we cannot count on any automatic or "benevolent" protection from our own meanness or folly in the period when man is directing his evolution. The most unsentimental thing in nature is nature itself. Anthony Eden, speaking of economics, once reminded the British people that there is no international welfare state. Neither is there a cosmic welfare state. If man can direct the course of his own evolution, he can also bring about his own extinction. Homo sapiens has probably not yet survived as long as did other kinds of "homines" whose branches have already died.

Man holds in his hands and in his mind the direction of his own evolution. Only individual human beings have hands and minds. The *individual* is the organism. But the individual's ecology is culture, and his most important environment is human society. Culture is the individual's ecology because the human being is almost bereft of instinct; of all animal life, he has the longest period of dependency; he must learn almost everything; he can learn enormously; he can learn a great many things and in a great many ways; and he learns always in and through a particular culture. Society is the individual's most important environment, because for the fulfillment of his purposes he needs the co-operation of other human beings. This is so even in his dealings with physical nature. It is so in a higher and more subtle way in the realization of his emotional, mental and spiritual purposes. Here we approach the issue of the individual and the society.

The basic invention of evolution was that of the many-celled organism. This made possible specialization of parts and functions, with a discovery of larger purposes and a greater "knowledge" of environment in the achievement of purposes.

One consequence is death. Death entered the world with the many-celled organism. The single-celled organism reproduces by division. Two cells resulting from a division are at the same time one another's mother, daughter and other self. One individual cell or many individual cells may die, but the protoplasm is immortal, in a terrestrial sense. But when, in a many-celled organism, the whole is dependent upon the functioning of specialized parts (skin, kidney, heart), the destruction of an essential part means the disorganization of the organism. Death is the price we pay for the complexity which makes consciousness possible. For this gift, death is a small price to pay.

Another consequence is greater variety. A single cell in division reproduces exact "descendants." With the mating of many-celled organisms, the result is an exchange of and an addition to genetic possibilities. This reaches its highest point in man. J. N. Spuhler estimates that there are between twenty thousand and forty-two thousand gene-loci in the human chromosomes. Taking thirty thousand as an average, two individuals coming together open up genetic possibilities in the number of two raised to the thirty-thousandth power. Weston La Barre[2] has written: ". . . all the human beings who have ever lived . . . have not scratched the surface of possible gene combinations in *Homo Sapiens.*" Consider this incredible number. Consider the different experiences that condition individuals. Consider the different reactions which individuals have even to the same experience. The individual—each individual —is literally a unique person.

About the age of two a tremendous development comes about in the human being. It is an identity of self. I know a three-year-old girl named Susan. I mistakenly called her Sally the other day. She was fiercely angry at me and troubled. She seemed to feel that in giving her the wrong name I was threatening to rob her of her identity.

The growth of this identity of self has an inner and outer expression. Inwardly it is an opening awareness, discovery and understanding of self—the "I." Outwardly it is the ability to relate to other human beings—the "Thou." The self is the organizing function by means of which the individual can relate himself to others: to "see himself as others see him"; to see himself in others, through empathy, sympathy, compassion; to discover common humanity; to find and live in the "We."

The ruthless forces of entropy—of dissolution—work ceaselessly on the physical organism. Whether they work also (short of senescence and death) upon the mind and personality depends on whether one takes command of the development of awareness.

The development of awareness is neither automatic nor random. It depends, first, on the individual himself, his vigilance, self-discipline, affirmation and effort; second, on the

[2] *The Human Animal* (Chicago, The University of Chicago Press) 1954, p. 97. La Barre refers to Spuhler, same page. Spuhler's paper is "On the Number of Genes in Man," *Science* CVIII (1948), pp. 279–80.

possibilities within the cultural ecology and the social environment. Now I turn to society.

In one sense the society is an abstraction, just as the "group" is an abstraction. Society is not an organism. The individual is not a cell in a system, the way our blood corpuscles are cells in the human organism. Only individual human beings feel, think, dream, plan and relate. In another sense society is a reality. It is a reality because human beings are the environment of each; because the idea of society is in the minds of individuals; because they must work together in order to cope with nature; because they need one another in order to realize their unique human selves and their common humanity.

At one and the same time individuals are each other's environment and are fellow human beings. The question is, which relationship is acted upon? Do they regard one another as "things" in an environment to be *used* for selfish purposes or as subordinate cells to be sacrificed for a social organism? Or do they regard one another as fellow human beings, their own "I's," our "Thou's," fellows in our common "We"? These questions introduce the related ideas of freedom and responsibility.

Man is conditioned by his environment, physical and social. But, actually or potentially, he is aware that he is being conditioned. This awareness is the embryo of freedom. Between the stimulus and the response "falls the shadow." He can pause in this shadow and throw his weight in behalf of one response and against another. He cannot only count to ten, but he can "count ten." Even more, he, alone and with others, can create the circumstances which produce the stimuli he desires to respond to. The more self-awareness a person has, the greater is his capacity to break the chain that binds response to stimuli, to create stimuli, and to create the stimuli he prefers. The more self-awareness that is shared by individuals, the greater their capacity to do this with and for one another.

A responsible person is one who acts (and in our responsible moments we *do* act) with regard to the wholeness and complexity of his own nature and the nature of everything. An irresponsible person is one who follows (and in our irresponsible moments we *do* follow) a minor impulse or potentiality at the expense of the richness and complexity of his total being.

Freedom and responsibility are two ends of the same staff, and a staff cannot have one end only. Melville (who did not share the optimism of the nineteenth century) wrote "Freedom is that which is not free," meaning free to be capricious or malignant. We are free only to do what we ought to do. But we must be free in order to discover the "ought." And to discover, we must explore. To explore is to get lost and err. But to err is oftentimes to learn. Indeed, error, reflected upon, is the greatest teacher. On the other end, responsibility has no meaning in a moral sense if one is not free to make choices, the wrong ones as well as the right.

A free society *relates* freedom and responsibility; a society which is not free tries to *separate* them and destroys both.

A free society does not require conformity. Indeed, it cannot, because the capacity to relate to others depends on the discovery of self, and each self is unique. To use a mechanical analogy, the equilibrium of a free society depends to a great extent on the inclusion of opposites. To use a biological analogy, the potentialities and actualities of social life are invigorated and widened by the exchange of individuality. We cannot often be sure which maverick is merely a fool or a pest or a danger, and which is the bringer of great gifts. Even when we think we are sure, we should remember that the hair shirt of individuality (like death for awareness) is the price we pay for a free society—a price we should gladly pay.

We should resist efforts to make us conform against our sense of individuality. But equally we should resist the temptation to force others to conform against theirs. This is a subtle thing. In *Archy and Mehitabel* there is the song of a worm being swallowed by a bird. At first he objects. But soon he cries, "I am beginning to think like the bird!" We are most in danger of losing our own individuality when we conspire with those who are like us against those who are different from us.

A free society has been described as one which has *shared* purposes, *shared* power and *shared* respect. A free society has been called an *open* society. It is, rather, an *opening* society, like a spiral inviting the infinite possibilities of man.

All the human race is today the social environment of each human being. The free society of the United States is today in competition with the closed, if not *closing*, society of the Soviet Union. This is a much more serious competitor than was Nazi Germany. It appeals to the real concept of the human race, not the spurious concept of a national race. It wears the smile of benevolence. It has challenged us to compete in helping other peoples improve, construct and advance, and to prove our intentions by domestic example. We must indeed have lost faith in ourselves if we fear this kind of competition. Which system, despite our imperfections, is really based on a belief in the individual on the one hand and the human race on the other? Which knows better how to solve the problems of production, both of food and machines? Which can help others to solve these problems without entoiling them?

All we need to do so is to care enough to join fully in the competition and to recover our confidence sufficiently to do so with enjoyment.

Returning to the United States in 1907, overdelicate, queasy Henry Adams wrote to his sister: "Curiosity is fairly fascinated by the sense of the immensity of the chance, and by the sense that the whole of the chance has been taken." In adopting self-government as our ideal and in extending suffrage to all adults, the American people *have* taken the *whole* chance. We can't "cash in" or "hedge our bets." We've got to *win*. But we are in a game which never ends. It doesn't even keep the same stakes. The stakes increase. Walt Whitman, who *did* share the optimism of the nineteenth century, nevertheless saw this. He wrote:

Have past struggles succeeded?
What has succeeded: yourself? your nation? nature?
Now understand me well—it is provided in the essence of
    things that from any fruition of success, no matter what,
    shall come something to make a greater struggle necessary.

Problem-solving therefore is not enough. The solution of one problem creates more than one and probably larger problems. Life's invention of the many-celled organism solved many problems—and created others. The genetic invention of man's brain solved many problems and created more. We cannot and should not hope to *eliminate* problems. That would be death. But we can hope to raise them to a higher level or to advance to larger problems. For the essence of life is purpose, and the process of life is the discovery of larger purposes through inventions. The most significant invention for man is his invention of a new type of evolution in which he is free through his mind to direct his future evolution.

Liberal education is education for the responsible use of that freedom.

In the human organism, the only cells which do not specialize and therefore lose some capacities at the price of gaining others are the genes. They can reproduce the whole person, and each person a unique person. One of man's distinctions from other animals is that he has never become so specialized as to become helpless with a change of environment. He *invents* special aids; he *develops* special functions. But he is able to put off these special tools as he wishes and return or advance to his general capacities.

Liberal education has relevance for all special functions of man, but, in itself, it is a return to or, better, an advancement to our common humanity. Liberal education is the effort to discover the larger purposes which distinguish man. Liberal education is the effort to prepare man to fulfill these larger purposes.

Liberal education is concerned not with thinkers as such or books as such, but with important issues: issues like non-life and life, life and death, space and time, form and process, justice and injustice, equality and inequality, freedom and responsibility, the individual and the society. Who is not concerned about such issues as these? Who is not capable at some level of wrestling with them? Who cannot be helped by a familiarity with the best that has been thought about these issues? Who would not profit by an orderly exchange of thoughts on them with others?

These are the most useful thoughts man can think—provided usefulness is defined largely enough, and provided that life and man are regarded as ends in themselves. For they are addressed to the purpose of human life, which is to fulfill itself, both as a unique individual and as a unique species. The difficulty does not lie in the issues. It lies in how they are put and in the lack of education or the miseducation of individuals to grapple with them.

h. w. prentis, jr.

The Concrete and the Abstract *

THE REAL PROFESSIONAL SCHOOL OF BUSINESS IS FOUND directly in the field of industrial and commercial life. Its permutations and combinations are unlimited in number; its pharmacopoeia is not stocked with standard remedies; its ruling statutes cannot be crystallized in codified form; its practice and procedure cannot be reduced to the mathematical equations of engineering formulae; its charts and compasses and chronometers cannot be synchronized. Could there be any better reasons than these why education of exceptional breadth and length and depth is required to sail its uncharted courses?

Here, it seems to me, we approach the kernel of the whole question of the value of a liberal education for business and industry. As President Lowell of Harvard University said years ago: "Dealing with the concrete does not lead to knowledge of the abstract." The inability to see a situation in the

* From "Liberal Education for Business and Industry," an address before the Conference of Industrial Leaders, Lake Arrowhead, California, May 24, 1958. By permission of the Estate of Henning W. Prentis, Jr.

large, the hesitancy of the vocationally trained mind to indulge in flights of imagination and thereby enlarge its scope, are not infrequently the result of the centripetal influence of professional education too closely focused and too narrowly applied. Lowell was right: "Dealing with the concrete does not lead to knowledge of the abstract." Consequently, we see too often electricians instead of electrical engineers; surveyors instead of civil engineers; mechanicians instead of mechanical engineers; conveyancers and pettifogging attorneys instead of lawyers; hack writers instead of real journalists; draftsmen instead of architects; pedagogues instead of professors; and impersonal, hair-splitting specialists instead of the old family doctor who was capable of sizing a patient up as a human being, not as a conglomeration of separate organs and glands! So by all means let us go as far as we can in the teaching of business as a profession, but in the same breath let us realize the vital importance of resourcefulness, constructive imagination and vision in modern business; then intensify the development of these characteristics through the broad stimulus that a liberal education affords. . . .

I came to the conclusion years ago that any man could claim to be liberally educated—whether he attended college or not—if, first, he had a storehouse of facts; second, he had trained his mind to think straight; third, he had acquired mental humility; and fourth, he had developed within himself a sense of the fitness of things which we in business call judgment.

A storehouse of facts: I mention this first because it seems to me that perhaps it is the least important in itself. Certainly, however, no man can lay claim to being liberally educated unless he has stowed away in his mind a certain mass of information about men and things. In my own case I have never had occasion to use for any practical purposes what little I ever knew about binomial theorems, integral calculus, the periodic law in chemistry, the Mendelian theory of inheritance, the choral odes in Greek tragedies, the scanning of Latin verse, the quantitative theory of money, the intricacies of Anglo-Saxon roots, the history of the Hyksos kings in Egypt, or the details of the plot of *Othello*—but all have affected my enjoyment of life and I am sure have aided me in developing any bit of mental resourcefulness or imagination that I may possess.

The ability to think straight: How rare an accomplishment this is and yet how vitally important if a man is to succeed in any business or profession. If education has failed to give a businessman the ability to analyze a given problem, that is, to break down the facts in any situation so that he can see the component parts clearly; and then to synthesize, to put together the clearly revealed facts as they stand out before him, in the proper patterns to form new concepts leading to logical conclusions, then I maintain that he can lay no just claim to being a really educated man. The mental discipline of a liberal education helps substantially in the acquirement of such ability.

Mental humility: If I were asked to pick out the one paramount benefit that a liberal education should bestow on a businessman, I should place mental humility—tolerance for other people's opinions—above all others. My personal observation indicates that the so-called self-made man finds this factor of tolerance more difficult to acquire than any other characteristic of a liberally educated mind. It is not surprising that this should be the case, because the man who has had to learn all of his lessons in the bitter school of experience naturally is prone to reason that, having achieved his goal, the only road by which it can be attained is the one particular route that he has laboriously traveled. As a matter of fact, his course may have been a very devious one, full of blind alleys from which he extricated himself only by the time-hallowed trial-and-error method. Someone else, meanwhile, may have found a far better road to the same objective, just as we see today the crooked highways of the past being straightened out for the dense motor transport of the future. Nothing could be more fatal to mental progress than such an attitude. A little knowledge *is* a dangerous thing. . . . "Knowledge is proud that it knows so much; wisdom is humble that it knows no more." Cowper's adage applies with peculiar force to those of us in business and industry. The closed mind of the businessman who thinks he knows it all insulates him from the constructive suggestions and criticisms of his associates and thereby paves the way for his own ultimate failure. . . .

A sense of the fitness of things, as I employ the term, is not mere social polish or intellectual veneer. It permeates a man's whole being. It leads him intuitively to reject the spurious and the false, to welcome the genuine and the true; to repulse baseness and vulgarity, and welcome nobility and refinement in thought, emotion and action. There is a Hindu saying that "knowledge, like water, takes the form of the vessel into which it is poured." Education that does not mold the character of the human receptacle, spiritually and morally, is readily transformed into lethal poison for the individual and social dynamite for the body politic.

Our gross neglect of liberal education for the past three generations is principally responsible for the social dynamite that lies all around us in fearful proximity to the lighted fuses of domestic demagogues and foreign fanatics bent on the destruction of our free institutions. With fatuous complacency we have steadily cut ourselves off from the intellectual and spiritual sources from which our freedom stems: the Greek philosophy of what constitutes a good life; the ancient Roman concept of civic virtue based on a government of laws, not of men; the Christian ideal of the infinite worth of the individual in the eyes of a sovereign God, which all of the collectivists deny.

These basic principles are the wellsprings of the liberal tradition from which flows our triune system of constitutional representative democracy, private competitive business, and civil and religious freedom. Liberal education in the classic sense of that phrase is the sole source from which these fountainheads of American freedom can be renewed. For well-nigh a century now we have been placing less and less emphasis on the study of religion and classical history, the philosophy of Plato and Aristotle; the writings of Cicero, the works of the great English political theorists of the seventeenth and eighteenth centuries; and the profound discussions of political philosophy by the founders of our own nation.

On the other hand, we have constantly given more and more emphasis to the physical side of life, forgetting that "dealing with the concrete does not lead to knowledge of the abstract." We have thereby lost the crusading faith in our free institutions which characterized the early days of this Republic. Meanwhile, the virus of collectivism turned loose on the world by Karl Marx in 1848 has done its fateful work. A host of our own people have fallen victims, and wittingly or unwittingly have become carriers of its deadly infection into our churches, schools and labor organizations and even into our government itself. The cancer of state socialism has already eaten far deeper into the American body politic than most of us realize.

Local responsibility for local affairs is essential to the preservation of the American Republic. This poses another question. And that is, how far specialization can be carried in business and professional life and still leave a man a fit citizen of a free society. A representative democracy is the hardest sort of government to operate because it requires the intelligent participation of a very large percentage of its citizenry to be successful. Furthermore, and this becomes increasingly evident as our civilization becomes more complex, popular self-government calls for a much broader base of general knowledge and sound perspective than the type of government where all a citizen has to do is to take orders. In other words, a free society requires resourceful citizens, men who can create their own environment, men who can look beyond the immediate present and judge a governmental policy on its long-range implications rather than on its short-term significance. The more the average man concentrates on a specialized job and his own affairs, the less capable he is apt to be as a citizen, and the more likely he is to lose his freedom. The highly specialized animals of prehistoric times perished because they could not control their environments on the one hand, or adapt themselves to changed conditions on the other. There is a significant lesson here for all of us who really want to keep our compass set in the right direction and maintain a free America. For if we permit ourselves to become so engrossed in our own specialized form of business or professional activity as to inhibit our securing a broad understanding of the fundamentals on which a free society like ours must rest, our free institutions are doomed to extinction as surely as those previous attempts at self-government "which have had their day and gone into the night."

To avoid this dire eventuality, we sorely need a sweeping and speedy revival of the type of liberal education for which our colleges and universities were so noted in the early days of the Republic. A well-informed, articulate, courageous citizenry is indispensable to the maintenance of political, intellectual, economic and spiritual freedom. Hence, liberal education for business and industry will be indeed a hollow mockery if it does not include the broadest possible understanding of, and training in, the responsibilities of citizenship in a republic of free men. . . .

charles a. nelson

The Liberal Arts in Management *

IN JUST THE LAST FEW YEARS THERE HAVE BEEN DEVELOPED a number of interesting liberal-education programs for the executive. These programs differ from one another, but they all have two characteristics in common: (1) they are devoted exclusively to liberal education, and (2) they are held exclusively for executives (with occasional exceptions at Aspen, Colorado). Their purpose is *not* vocational training. Rather, their aim is explicitly to disengage the executive from his day-to-day problems and to engage him instead in studies which do not immediately affect his company's balance sheet or his own executive performance. If in some cases they have had

* From the *Harvard Business Review* (May-June, 1958). By permission of the *Harvard Business Review*.

an immediate occupational effect, both the educators and the businessmen involved, I think, would agree that none of them should be *judged* by their momentary practical application. In this sense they are different from those excellent programs, offered generally by business schools, which are designed to strengthen and deepen the executive's knowledge about specific business subjects.

It is a tribute to the wisdom of business leaders that such efforts can have been undertaken without prior guarantee from the educators that short-term advantages to the companies involved would result. It is also a tribute to the integrity of the educators involved that they have had the courage to proceed with their programs of liberal education, which in most cases have made no real concessions to the practical bent of mind that generally characterizes the modern business executive.

Now that a few years have passed, businessmen and educators alike are starting to wonder what the fruits of these interesting endeavors will be.

The two terms *management* and *the liberal arts* are both very fluid in their meaning. If there is any tendency on the part of business managers to suppose that the educators are all in agreement on what they mean by the liberal arts, that notion should be dispelled at once. If, on the other hand, the educators suppose that educators are in agreement on what they mean by management and the functions of the manager, that notion should also be dispelled. Since our society is full of change, revolution and surprises, education and business as two of the fundamental activities of our society are always in transition, and words in common use are often differently understood.

We are dealing with two notions customarily thought to be quite remote from one another. We tend to think of the liberal arts as elevated, impractical and theoretical. We think of management as down to earth, realistic and practical. We feel that management, as Peter F. Drucker has said, "is not concerned with knowledge for its own sake; it is concerned with performance."[1] Conversely, we say that the liberal arts, in effect, are not concerned with performance; they are concerned with knowledge for its own sake. But when we examine this dichotomy more closely, I believe we shall see that the liberal arts are actually very much concerned with performance of a certain kind and that this kind of performance is of the highest importance to management.

To help our examination, let me introduce two other terms—*art* and *science*. Art is a clue to the meaning of the liberal arts. Science has been associated with management ever since the

[1] *The Practice of Management* (New York, Harper & Brothers, 1954), p. 353.

pioneering work of Frederick Taylor, the father of "scientific management."

The root meaning of art is "to make." Those activities most properly called arts are the activities of making, in which something material in nature, such as wood or stone, is given shape, is made into something that has a new form. Thus we see that the sculptor and painter, and the carpenter and mechanic as well, are each engaged in a form of art. By extension, the term art has come to be applied to many other things, such as the dramatic arts, the art of persuasion, the "lively" arts and so on.

But no matter how the term has been extended, it always carries with it the suggestion of some kind of activity—some form of doing or making. Does this sense of the word lose all its meaning when we turn to the liberal arts? It would appear that it does only if the liberal arts cannot be thought to be useful or practical. As we shall see, they *can*—and should—be thought of this way. But first let us define science, the other term.

Science, at root, simply means knowledge. Thus, when we speak of physics, chemistry and biology as natural sciences, we mean that each of them contains a body of knowledge about an aspect of nature. This is a different use of the term than we employ when we speak of "the scientific method" or "the scientific attitude." By the scientific method we mean a way of arriving at the knowledge which makes up the body of the science. When we speak of the scientific attitude, we mean a quality of character in the scientist—in the one who seeks knowledge—which determines his personal approach to his work; it consists of objectivity and devotion to truth.

Now we can state a relationship between art and science. Science is knowledge; art is the creative and skillful application or reshaping of knowledge. Thus, for every art there must be an underlying science. If the liberal arts are actually arts, some knowledge underlies them. Similarly, when we think of management as a practical activity, we think of it as an art; behind it lies a science—a body of knowledge about management.

What are the liberal arts, and what knowledge do they apply? The liberal arts have a long tradition. Going back at least as far as the second century before Christ, there were seven liberal arts: grammar, rhetoric, logic, arithmetic, geometry, music and astronomy. These terms, however, mean very different things now than they did originally; without elaborate interpretation they would not seem to us to be a complete list of what we call the liberal arts. Ralph Barton Perry gives a more familiar list when he says that the liberal studies par excellence are literature and the fine arts, history, religion and philosophy. He adds:

Education is liberal in so far as it invites and qualifies men to choose deeply and fundamentally, to choose ends as well as means, to choose remote as well as immediate ends, to choose from many rather than from few possibilities. . . .

If it is asked *why* these studies are liberating, the reason is that they stimulate the imagination, create perspective and breadth of outlook, and thus call into play the faculty of choice.[2]

The liberal studies themselves are the sciences, or the bodies of knowledge, which underlie the liberal arts. The knowledge of the elements of language, for example, we call the science of grammar. The skillful and creative application of this knowledge is an art—the art of writing. Since one has to have the knowledge before one can apply it, a man can acquire the art of writing only by mastering the knowledge of language.

Liberal education, then, leads to the liberation of a man through two kinds of activity: the acquisition of knowledge and the practice of the arts which depend on that knowledge.

Those studies are liberal which help to perfect a man *as a man*. This gives us a distinction between liberal and vocational education, since vocational studies tend to perfect men not as men but as carpenters or machinists or doctors or managers. Vocational subjects can be more or less liberal depending upon the way in which they are taught and the nature of the vocation for which they are the preparation, since some vocations are more consistent with the full development of man's potentialities than others.

We can readily see, then, why the advocates of the liberal arts often insist that these arts are not useful or practical. They want to emphasize that the liberal arts are debased when they are used merely to help a man earn a living. But what they mean to say is that the liberal arts are in reality the most useful of all arts because they help to fulfill the highest of all human purposes—the perfection of a man as an individual.

The liberal-arts teacher is understandably somewhat uneasy when he finds the liberal arts clutched in the embrace of industry. He fears that the affair is illicit and that the liberating breath will be squeezed out of the arts. He may protest that his mistress is not to be bought, yet he is secretly pleased, too, that she is found so attractive to strangers.

But why should executives be interested in the liberal arts? Courtney C. Brown, dean of the Graduate School of Business at Columbia, and formerly assistant to the chairman of the board of the Standard Oil Company (New Jersey), sets forth four reasons why the liberal arts will become increasingly important to business. Briefly summarized, they are as follows:

[2] See pages 46, 48.

(1) The liberal arts nourish those qualities of a free society in which an enterprise can best flourish—"broad comprehension, the ability to undertake appraisal in a calm, deliberate manner, an ordered capacity for reason, a sense of toleration, and a critical inquisitiveness."

(2) The liberal arts counteract the narrowing effects of specialization.

(3) The liberal arts contribute to an understanding of the complex problem of "managing people."

(4) The liberal arts help to develop the executive's capacity for self-expression—a necessary skill because of the position of increasing political and intellectual leadership in which the businessman finds himself.[3]

To appreciate more fully how the liberal arts apply to management, and to what extent, let us look at the manager's job in more detail. We shall find, I think, that the relationship between the liberal arts and the successful practice of management is even more intimate than has so far been supposed.

What I intend to establish is that the liberal arts are not merely a collection of added skills which the manager will find useful to draw on from time to time as situations arise calling for a broad-gauge public speech or the development of company policies displaying an enlightened view of the interdependence of public policy and business success. Those are secondary values. My view is that the liberal arts, when they become an integral part of managers' thinking, transform the practice of management and even change its whole character. In the process the liberal arts are not made subservient tools; they retain, as nearly as is possible in any practical enterprise, their meaning as worthy ends in themselves.

While much has been written about the various aspects of management, its general nature and the task of the manager have not received a great deal of attention. Perhaps Drucker gives this the most fruitful treatment when he writes that at the heart of management's work is the obligation "to make a productive enterprise out of human and material resources."[4] If we take "productive enterprise" to mean an economic organ devoted to the production of goods or services, and if we take the "human resources" to include both managers and workers, I think we can use this definition as inclusive of all of management's functions of which Drucker speaks.

Note the use of the verb "to make" and the phrase "out of human and material resources." Our earlier discussion suggests at once that what we are talking about is an art. Furthermore,

[3] Courtney C. Brown, in *The Saturday Review* (November 21, 1953), p. 36.
[4] *Op. cit.*, p. 12.

it must be a complicated art, for not only does it involve material resources, as does sculpture or carpentry, but it involves human resources as well. And these human resources have a unique importance, as Drucker points out:

> The enterprise, by definition, must be capable of producing more or better than all the resources that comprise it. It must be a genuine whole: greater than—or at least different from—the sum of its parts with its output larger than the sum of all input.
>
> The enterprise cannot therefore be a mechanical assemblage of resources. To make an enterprise out of resources it is not enough to put them together in logical order and then to throw the switch of capital as the nineteenth-century economists firmly believed (and as many of their successors among academic economists still believe).
>
> What is needed is a transmutation of the resources and this cannot come from an inanimate resource such as capital. It requires management.
>
> But it also is clear that the resources capable of enlargement can only be human resources. All other resources stand under the laws of mechanics. They can be better utilized or worse utilized but they can never have an output greater than the sum of the input. On the contrary the problem in putting nonhuman resources together is always to keep to a minimum the inevitable output shrinkage through friction, etc. Man alone of all the resources available to man can grow and develop.[5]

We can gain some insight into the meaning of this for the modern manager if we look at the work of the artisan. A carpenter takes wood, shapes it, and makes a house. His art consists in his control over the material—the wood. The knowledge he requires is the knowledge of the properties of the material he shapes.

In industry we have production workers who perform similar functions with the aid of time-saving machinery. But the *manager* in charge has to deal with both human and material resources. The knowledge that he requires is therefore knowledge of material *and* of men. We are becoming increasingly aware of the difference it makes to the productivity of any enterprise if the human beings in it are well or badly managed. Unfortunately, the habits of the old arts of handling material have tended to carry over to the management of men, which accounts for the phrase "handling men" with its implication that men are to be manipulated and used as if they were leather or wood.

Materials can be handled. Men must be taught. We have failed to see that the art of teaching is part of the art of the

[5] *Ibid.*

manager. We have thought of teaching as one profession and of management as another. I suggest that a manager must become a good teacher if he is to be a good manager. To see how teaching infuses the practice of management, let us take a very simple example:

A shoemaker by himself possesses a knowledge of leather and shoes; his art of shoemaking is a product of this knowledge and of his skill in shaping the shoe according to a pattern in his mind or on a paper before him. But if he becomes an entrepreneur, he must hire a number of men with various degrees of skill to make shoes under his direction. Each of these men must acquire the knowledge and skill of shoemaking.

How is our businessman-shoemaker to transmit this knowledge and skill? He can do it by going through the motions of the job himself, by description, by written instructions and by other devices, depending on how ingenious he is and how complicated the process is. In so doing, he teaches. A manager or foreman may be many things, but he must be a teacher. What does he have to know in order to teach? He has to know not only the qualities of the leather and the patterns of the shoes, but he has to know something about men, since it is men he is teaching.

Teaching is an art which combines the transmitting of a knowledge of some subject (in our example, shoemaking) with the artful use of another knowledge which pertains to the student (in this case, the men who are making shoes). Teaching always combines these elements. As a result, it is perfectly possible to have a completely knowledgeable man who is a poor teacher because, while he has knowledge of the subject and even a theoretical knowledge of men and how they learn, he may not have developed the art of combining the knowledge and transmitting it successfully to others. The problem of mastering this art is perhaps as great in universities as it is in industry.

Now, to take our example one more step:

Let us suppose that our entrepreneur shoemaker builds a factory and hires several men under him to perform the functions he formerly carried out, namely, supervising other men who make the shoes. Now we begin to get the pattern of management in its full complexity. Our shoemaker must acquire a new knowledge and a new skill, for he must develop among his new subordinates the same kinds of teaching skills which formerly enabled him to teach workers how to make shoes. He has become a manager who manages not only the workers and their work but other managers as well.

How does he carry this job out? Again, partly through the teaching function. Now he must not merely teach men how to perform some physical task, but teach them how to teach what they know to others. This is a large element of the art of managing managers. As our shoemaker becomes more removed from the making of the product, his task becomes increasingly complex. His knowledge is broadened, and his art is more and more concerned with men and less and less with shoes.

What determines whether or not the manager learns what is taught him? Obviously, his native capacity to learn is one important factor, but two others are also vital: whether or not he can see the usefulness to him of what is being taught; and whether or not what he is asked to learn is consistent with the policies and practices of the company as he sees them from day to day.

This is another way of saying that what a man learns from his boss depends a great deal on what the boss *does*. The boss may think he is teaching when he speaks or writes memos. He may not realize that he is teaching when he hires, promotes, fires and otherwise decides important company matters. And the manager under him may not realize consciously that he is being taught by these actions, but there is no doubt that he learns from them.

Any discussion of the education of managers or of management development will proceed from far too narrow a base if it fails to note that the "learning situation" of the manager consists predominantly of the actions and decisions of his immediate superior and of the general organization and policies of the company. We must take this into account later when we consider the relationship of university-centered programs to the development of managers.

Looking at the manager's functions in this way highlights the distinction between the roles of science and art. Thus Frederick Taylor's contribution to what he called "scientific management" was the analysis of work into all its component motions. But, as Drucker points out, he made the mistake of interpreting this analysis to mean that each motion should be performed by a different worker. As a result, Taylor's work spurred the development of the early type of mass production which permitted assembly-line workers a very small amount of variation in their methods of work.

However, studies subsequent to his time have shown that this is not the most productive organization of work. The results do not demonstrate any defect in the science, in the analysis of the nature of the work to be done. The defect was in the art, in the application of Taylor's analysis to the organization of the work without any regard to the characteristics of the worker.[6]

[6] See Peter F. Drucker, *op. cit.*, pp. 282 ff.

When it is said by the critics of scientific management that management can never be a science, what they really mean is that management must always be both science and art, both knowledge and the creative and skillful application or reshaping of knowledge. Thus, successful practice of the art always requires judgment, balance, the weighing of alternatives, the understanding of the complexities, the consideration of both material and human consequences. The successful practice of management requires that the frontiers of both the science and the art be continually explored; for the practice of the art provides the necessary knowledge for scientific analysis, and the scientific knowledge in turn sets the sure base from which the art must proceed.

But there is more to management than efficiency and production. There is also the question of how it affects the managers themselves. A grave responsibility follows from the fact that most of the productive energies of managers for most of their productive years are under the guidance of the company. There is a tendency for those who hold the more responsible positions to carry much heavier burdens of work than those in less responsible positions. It is not uncommon for the presidents and vice-presidents of our corporations to make practically a whole way of life out of their work, while it is fairly common among those in lower management positions to be geared to a forty- or forty-five-hour week and to engage in completely different and separate activities outside the office.

With some exceptions we can say that the more management responsibilities a person has, the more management tends to become a whole way of life. To the extent that this is so every manager owes it to himself to make the best kind of life he can out of his work, for so much of his life is bound up in it.

But the top executive also has a broader, more general responsibility. All of us do many things purely out of necessity; they are part of making a living. We do other things that we recognize as being good in themselves, some of which we do as a part of our job, to the extent that we can make of our work a series of events or decisions which are worthy in themselves and which we would be proud to engage in whether for money or not. To that extent we should make management an activity worthy of a man as a man.

It was a university administrator, Robert M. Hutchins, who saw clearly the moral character of the management job when he said:

Habits are formed by action. The way to become a good administrator is to administer. This is also the way to become a bad administrator: for vice is a habit too. The minimum function of the administrator is to decide, and, since he has to make more decisions than most men, he has the chance to be either an especially good or an especially bad man.[7]

Most executives' decisions at the top level affect other managers—their lives, their satisfactions in their work and their ability to perform the kind of job they can be proud of. It is possible to organize a company in such a way as to maximize every opportunity to achieve these satisfactions. It is also possible to organize a company in which the opposite occurs—in which men are almost of necessity made worse because of their association with the corporation. Executives have it within their power to frustrate the creative energies of most of the men under their direction or to help them to fulfill their capacities.

It was the moral imperative of Immanuel Kant, the German philosopher, that every man must be treated as an end in himself. This means that men are not tools to be "handled," for tools are implements for some other end. Is there any way that this moral idea can be made consistent with the idea of a corporation in which work is done through men? I can think of only one way—and it is an imperfect one. This is to attempt to design each man's job in such a way that he fully comprehends it, that he sees it as a job worthy of him as a man, that he does it of his own choice, and that he is permitted to take the responsibility for his acts and to develop the moral fiber that comes from accepting the consequences of his decisions.

An examination of the jobs that are available in any organization will make us appreciate that this can never be perfectly realized. But is it not realistic to make it a goal?

To management thus conceived, the liberal arts contribute an understanding of the nature and aims of men and the conditions under which men are able to achieve what they seek. They can enable the manager to see more clearly the occasions on which the objectives and activities of the corporation are likely to conflict with the aims and the purposes of the men who must carry out those objectives. And the object of the manager will be to keep these conflicts to a minimum and, when they do arise, to reduce as much as is within his power the adverse effects of the conflicts.

The liberal arts also contribute to the manager's understanding of his function as a teacher. The foregoing analysis suggests that an art is a kind of making or creating. The manager teaches through action, decision and organization at least as much as he does by instruction. And his teaching concerns both knowledge and morals.

In effect, the art of management is itself an imperfect liberal

[7] From a speech delivered on April 23, 1946.

art. The liberal arts are concerned with the making of men. Properly speaking, they are pursued for their own sake; thus, we do not think of them as occupations, as we do of the industrial arts (mechanics, carpenters, pattern makers and so on). However, some occupations can coincide closely with the exercise of an art for its own sake. It depends on how they are performed. For instance, a writer can write something that has a merit of its own, or he can grind out work in order to get paid. Presumably, every writer who gets paid for his work does something of each. Again, many teachers are concerned with the liberal arts; and teaching, generally speaking, is thought of as a high calling because it is concerned with the making of men. Yet we know that within the profession of teaching there are also some who teach only to make money, not to make men; they get little reward either way.

We may say that the worth-whileness of any art depends on the intrinsic value of the product and on the excellence with which the work is done. The manager has the task of carrying forward the objectives of the productive enterprise in which he works; in doing so he must inevitably teach, well or badly. To the extent that he teaches well, through what he does and what he says, he advances the true interests of the men under his direction as well as his own interest.

Of course, most managers do not see themselves as teachers, and few managers seem to remember, at the critical moments of decision, that every man must be treated as an end in himself. Because of these prevailing conditions, William H. Whyte, Jr., has argued that every man must "fight the Organization."[8] I would prefer to say that every man should be just beyond its reach. Sometimes he must fight; but in order to achieve the perspective from which he can see the proper course of action, he must stand off by himself. He must first of all be a man, self-contained. The practice of the liberal arts will help him to be such a man.

In Plato's *Republic* the discussion of justice in the state originates out of a desire to find justice in the man. It is suggested that by looking at the state one might discover the nature of justice, and then be in a position to apply it to justice in the individual, since things are "written larger" in a state than they are in a man. Plato comes to the conclusion that justice in the state consists in each class doing its own work. Later we find that the meaning of this for the individual is that each part of the man—reason, spirit and appetite—must do its own work under the rule of reason. I think it is fair to conclude (in opposition to all those who have tried to make a totalitarian of

[8] *The Organization Man* (New York, Simon and Schuster, Inc., 1956), p. 404.

Plato) that the just man in the just state must be ruled not only by the philosopher kings, but by his own reason as well.

May I suggest that a goal of the corporation and therefore of its manager might be to organize the company and its work so that each man in it may be ruled not only by the manager but by his own reason as well. Thus, as he helps to achieve the aims of the corporation, he also fulfills some of his aims as a man. We keep our perspective if we remember that Plato's state exists in idea only.

What are the consequences of the foregoing ideas for formal programs of liberal education for executives? In concluding, I would like to put forth a few constructive suggestions and expose to view some problems which need further exploration.

The exploration of ideas seems to take place best amid widely differing points of view held by different sorts of people. Yet businessmen, while by no means all alike, are more homogeneous than a group which includes doctors, lawyers, union leaders, churchmen and public officials. On what educational grounds do we justify the separation of the executive from all these other men?

There is, of course, a historical explanation. Most of the current interest in liberal-arts programs has stemmed from the top executives of large corporations. Having identified a problem (i.e., need for individual growth) and a possible solution (i.e., liberal-arts education), they have then characteristically gone about finding a direct means of trying out the approach, by providing the educational experience for their own executives through arrangements with a co-operative university. Thus, one finds a number of programs in which participation is limited not only to businessmen but, even more serious, to executives of one company.

The fact that such an arrangement is perfectly understandable does not necessarily make it a good one. If it lacks, as I think it may, some of the stimulus to be found in a more heterogeneous grouping, the universities should be encouraged to cast a wider net. This may involve some onerous promotional activities, since the additional participants sought will not be so readily found. For one thing, most of them—the lawyers and doctors and small businessmen—will have to pay their own way. Thus, it may be more difficult to maintain a tuition fee that fully supports the program. (However, I think such a fee should be maintained; this is not the kind of activity the university should have to subsidize.)

All arts, including the liberal arts, are developed by practice. They cannot be taken out of cold storage and skillfully brought to bear upon isolated problems. The liberal studies which underlie these arts can be pursued in formal programs, and so can the arts themselves to a limited extent; but they will only be realized in a man to the degree that they remake him as an individual. Inevitably this will remake him as a manager.

What can the colleges and universities do to ensure that their liberal-arts programs for executives have this pervasive effect on the men they enroll?

Two measures occur to me, both of which characterize at least a few of the programs now being carried on. One is to make the program as intensive as possible; this ensures maximum impact with a minimum of distraction by other continuing concerns. The other is to employ methods—particularly disciplined discussions—that place a premium on re-examination of opinions and prejudices by each man through reasoned argument. Once they are deeply ingrained, such rigorous habits of thought will persist and carry over into realms of judgment outside the formal setting of the program.

This raises a further question. We know that a liberal education is not something that can be fully acquired in college or in any adult formal program; it is a lifelong process. The liberal arts can never be fully mastered since their object is the perfection of the man. What can be done in formal programs to help to set habits of mind and action which will persist when the program ends? I think there are at least three ways in which more assurance can be had that these habits will persist:

(1) Instructors should be chosen and materials should be selected which make the pursuit of ideas exciting, so that the experience is relished, remembered with pleasure and carried forward with real anticipation.

(2) The methods of inquiry into the liberal studies should be opened up and clarified so that the adult can pursue his study independently with justified confidence. For example, if he is aware of the *methods* of the physicist, in addition to the main substantive ideas of the science, he will be better able to proceed on his own initiative with further reading and study. The principle applies equally well to poetry, logic or anthropology.

(3) The program should be deliberately organized so that it cannot be thought of as a terminal one. When the last class is over, great questions should be left hanging unanswered, and a healthy sense of urgent unfinished business should pervade the closing exercises.

As to what kind of knowledge ought to be taught, a manager needs an understanding not only of the particular men under his management but also of the nature of men in general. How can formal programs of liberal education best help to convey this knowledge of men to the executive?

I suggest, as one approach, that these programs should capitalize on the adult experience of the participants. The executive should be helped to interpret better his own "common-sense" knowledge of men. To this end, the programs would do well to direct attention to two fruitful sources of understanding in literature:

(1) The best discursive treatments of human nature should be examined in such disciplines as anthropology, philosophy, psychology, biology and religion.

(2) The other equally fruitful source is drama, the novel and poetry. Here, through such writers as Shakespeare, Aeschylus, Donne, and Fielding, perceptions of reality are sharpened, and as a result experience and theory are illuminated. The plight of King Lear, for example, both illuminates personal experience in the granting of power and favors and clarifies the generalizations of political theory such as one finds in Hobbes or Machiavelli.

In various current programs both sources are being employed successfully, and in a few cases they are given considerable emphasis.

As suggested earlier, the art of managing men depends in large part upon a kind of teaching. But the manager teaches as much by how he organizes, what he does, and what he permits the managers under him to do as he does by verbal or written instruction. How can formal programs of liberal education contribute to the development of this art among executives?

We must assume that the contribution of the programs will be limited in this respect because the art of teaching can be perfected only by practice. This does not mean, however, that nothing can be done about it. Before the art can be practiced consistently, it must be understood to *be* an art; and the nature of the art, with the relationship of the practice to the knowledge underlying practice, can be explored and discussed in many contexts in the course of a formal program of liberal education. Attention can be focused, for example, on the art of teaching, the art of writing, the art of sculpture, the art of conversation and the art of management.

Perhaps more important, the art of the teacher should be exemplified by as good models as the university can find for teaching in these programs. These teachers should personify the liberal arts, never perfectly realized, of course, but in advanced stages of individuality and maturity. Technical competence in

English literature, philosophy, or anthropology should serve merely to define the group from which the appropriate teachers should be chosen; the criterion for final selection should fulfill the aim of exhibiting the liberal arts alive through the many facets of character and intelligence of consistent, believable teachers—men in whom arts and sciences have come happily together.

Are such teachers rare and hard to find? Rare, indeed. We shall have to compromise. But is it not always useful when compromising to see clearly what we have compromised with?

Finally, liberal-arts programs involve certain risks—on the part both of companies and of universities, to say nothing of risks taken by the participating executives. The risk the company takes is that it supports an activity which may result in more change in its policies, practices and personnel than it has bargained for. The risk the university takes is that, being partly responsible for these changes, it may be misunderstood, perhaps distrusted. What actions can be taken to ensure that the risks are fully understood? And what can be done to make it likely that, once understood, the risks will continue to be accepted so that the liberal arts may come to infuse management to a degree far beyond our present hopes?

A full exchange of views should occur regularly between representatives of the corporations and representatives of the universities to ensure that the risks are understood. The expectations, the known results, the failures as well as the apparent successes, and the uncertainties should be discussed candidly. The corporation leaders need this exchange to enable them to understand and judge the participants from their companies. The university representatives need this exchange so that they will know as fully as possible the results of their labors, and so that they will be able to consider revisions in curriculum in the light of the best information.

To ensure that the risks will continue to be accepted, perhaps the most important admonition is that the process of liberal education should not be oversold or misrepresented. There are twin dangers: that the corporations should make such programs the gateways to promotion, and that the universities should see such corporate policies as proof of their programs' success. Who is prepared to say to what extent the liberal arts fit, or unfit, a man for corporate success according to the current definitions of business success? How many examples do we have of the liberal arts embodied in the business leaders of the day?

clarence b. randall

The Cultivation of the Mind *

THE ULTIMATE TEST OF ANY INTELLECTUAL DISCIPLINE IS NOT what it does for others, but what it achieves within the life of the particular individual. The cultivation of the mind and the illumination of the spirit are ends in themselves and bring their own rewards. Education is too precious a thing to be measured by a money index. Obviously it is important that each of us knows how to make a living, but that is not the ultimate purpose of life itself. Far more important than the making of the living is the living of the life; and the highest aim of all education must be to make life richer and fuller. As the man grows within himself, his company gains, and society gains, but it is that inner growth which must be the end sought.

Why do I believe that a liberal education fulfills this purpose more effectively than specialized training?

First of all, study of the humanities brings home to each of us the importance of creating a personal philosophy and trains us in the processes for achieving that end.

By personal philosophy I mean a scale of values which we ourselves consciously establish for the control of our conduct, and a motivation to which we respond.

Life would be drab and meaningless if a man did not set for himself certain goals and commit himself to some method for keeping score. Much of his efforts would otherwise be wasted. We need to know what we seek to accomplish with our lives; we need to establish principles to which we will give complete loyalty in the fulfillment of our purposes. Making the most from life requires that each of us brings to the fullest development those talents with which he is endowed at birth, and this cannot be done without purposes and standards.

This endowment of natural gifts varies among men. We cannot therefore pattern our conduct solely by reference to others; we must rather by reflection and self-analysis assess our own capabilities and consciously determine how best to employ them. Thus only do we live worthily.

* From *The Randall Lectures*. By permission of The Fund for Adult Education.

The establishment in one's life of such a personal philosophy can scarcely be advanced by the pursuit of technology. What is involved here is the whole study of man, and we advance our own self-analysis and our own thinking about ourselves by studying the similar processes of mind of those who have gone before.

We turn to history to learn of the accomplishments and the failures of others. We turn to literature and poetry because in them man has expressed his highest ideals and his deepest tragedies. We turn to the formal study of philosophy to learn with humility how the great minds of the ages have endeavored to analyze for all men the very problems with which each of us struggles. We turn to religion for the inspiration and guidance that come from glimpsing the relationship of the individual to the infinite and the unchanging.

Once a man recognizes the urgency of establishing in his own life a guiding philosophy, he recognizes that he is engaged in a lifetime project. The liberal-arts student who has chosen his courses wisely may have a head start over his contemporaries who have chosen the intellectual disciplines of the specialties, but the best of preparation for living can be hardly more than the beginning. Life is a succession of challenges to one's scale of values, and we grow by test and adjustment.

For this purpose we need a continuing and orderly interchange of ideas with those about us, through which, as we explore their minds, we reassess our own thinking.

This is not easy to achieve in modern life. The art of good conversation, for example, is dying out among us. Businessmen particularly live their lives at too mad a pace for the reflective processes to flourish; and, even under such opportunities as persist, our habits inhibit the vigorous interchange of thinking which characterized those earlier and slower days of our forefathers.

Even our recreations are stylized. Impressions come to us from without instead of being generated from within. Just as we tend to abandon physical exercise in favor of spectator sport, so we tend to abandon intellectual exercise in favor of the presentation of ideas by mechanical means. Each advance in the technology of the visual aids tends to soften our capacity to think for ourselves.

We businessmen take few pauses during the day for thinking on subjects of general interest. We either grab a sandwich at our desk without interrupting our work, or dash somewhere for lunch for the sole purpose of talking shop. Instead of dispersing into the community at noon, we establish executive dining rooms where we always see the same people. Inbreeding, therefore, is common in corporate management. At home our wives fear the impact of general conversation at social gatherings, and resort to some form of group activity that will not disclose the general incapacity for participating in stimulating conversation. Those who can talk are frustrated by those who refuse to listen.

One reason why the art of conversation is disappearing is that those who are specialists by education or employment tend to raise barriers among us. Frequently they are eloquent on their specialty and silent on all else. Good conversation requires common substance, on which all people are informed, and to which all can make a contribution by original thinking.

The only antidote to this is general education. If our complex modern society is to retain any semblance of homogeneity, all men must continuously strive so to cultivate their minds and broaden their outlooks that we may have common ground at the intellectual level for the interchange of ideas.

Just as good private conversation is entering into a period of decadence, so is vigorous public debate of the great issues of the day. That field has been taken over by a few professionals, and abandoned by the amateurs. Newspaper columnists and radio and television commentators do our debating for us, and few indeed are the businessmen who make important contributions to the forming of public opinion.

Among those who are articulate it will be found that the great majority had their training in the liberal arts. It takes an exceptional man indeed to develop late in life a talent for the forming of public opinion if his undergraduate training was spent in the laboratories, and if his adult life has been devoted to engineering or scientific pursuits. Many men who come to substantial business responsibility from the technical disciplines sense urgently the importance of being able to make their opinions felt, but sense it too late in their lives. A few by sheer will power achieve competence regardless of the years, but most find that learning to write and speak English effectively for the first time at middle life is like trying then to learn their first foreign language.

Yet many are the subjects on which we desperately need both private conversation and public debate in order to discharge our responsibilities as citizens. Nothing could be more urgent than our need to improve our understanding of the American way of life, and its chances of survival in a difficult world.

Chief among the subjects that need discussion and debate is the concept of freedom.

Daily this precious word passes our lips, yet few there are who could put into a crisp paragraph their concept of what

freedom means. It is solely because we do not fully understand freedom that we sometimes fail to recognize limitations
on freedom until great damage has been done. For the same
reason we often ignore abuses of freedom.

For example, I have always felt that freedom should be
expressed in dynamic terms. It is not a negative concept.
Freedom is doing. To express this greatest of human ideas
as freedom *from* something is a negative approach. If disease
or poverty or some unfortunate circumstance is removed from
the life of an individual, that is a definite good; but still it is
not freedom, unless, after the condition is removed, that individual exercises his talents to do something of positive benefit for mankind. To be able to do something worth while and
then to fail to make the effort cannot be real freedom.

I have heard it said that our great modern advance in
technology has brought great advance in freedom, but I doubt
that hypothesis. On the contrary, in many respects our new
technology has inhibited freedom. Take, for example, the
electronic listening device by which an operator a half-mile
away can listen in on a private conversation. Surely persons
conversing with candor, because they believe themselves to be
alone, are less free than if they were not spied upon.

And let us not forget that the Declaration of Independence,
the Bill of Rights and the Gettysburg Address, in which are
embodied some of the noblest concepts of freedom yet framed
by man, were conceived without the aid of technology.

I find no relationship between technology and freedom,
but believe rather that the advancement of the concept of
liberty rests entirely upon the cultivation of the mind and the
spirit of man through the processes of general education.

Let me turn now to the impact on society of the inner
growth of which I have spoken. What are its outward manifestations?

First of all, the man whose horizons have been widened
and sensibilities aroused by the exciting processes of liberal
education senses a continuing obligation to the community
about him. He is aware that education is a great privilege
which brings correlative responsibilities, and he seeks to fulfill this obligation by entering fully into all phases of his community life.

This was the tragedy of the Middle Ages. Individual scholars in that period of history often reached great heights of
erudition, but they were filled with fear and disgust by the
world about them. They therefore withdrew from society
and carried on their scholarly endeavors in solitude. As a
consequence the world which needed their light slipped further and further into darkness.

Today the broadly educated man must live worthily, or he denies his heritage. For those of us whose lives are spent in the service of corporations, this means that it is our obligation to see that they, too, live worthily.

The full significance of the corporation as an effective instrumentality of modern society is not fully evaluated by most Americans. In my view, its contribution to the present standards of life in our country is so unique that it might almost be regarded as synonymous with our level of civilization.

The genius of the corporation is that it provides a medium by which the savings of the many may safely and effectively be put to work voluntarily under the management of the few. This process has now gone so far in our country that in many publicly owned institutions the number of stockholders equals the number of employees.

No task is too great for some of our American companies. No plan is too bold, no requirement of capital too great for them to undertake, if the projects are rewarding.

Backward countries lack this working tool. They have no tradition of the pooling of individual savings for a common task, other than through government. They have no understanding of the equity form of ownership; on the contrary, they have great aversion toward permitting others to manage their affairs. As a consequence, the individual citizen who is thrifty has no recourse but to invest his savings in tangible purchases which he can watch.

For this reason initiative languishes, small industry does not start, and the State becomes the sole source of capital.

The power to control the lives of the citizens thus stands ready for the dictator. Freedom yields to economic power for lack of what is a common working tool with us, and the few may at any time dominate the mass.

No invention of modern times has contributed more to our well-being than this Anglo-Saxon concept of voluntary collective ownership based on limited liability.

The day has passed, however, when the corporation may be thought of merely as a legal entity. It is now also an instrumentality for social progress, and the management which is entrusted with the material well-being of the stockholders must be thought of also as the custodian of the collective social responsibility of the owners.

This is achieved through people. The corporation participates in the life of the community only through the lives of those who act for it. There is no other means by which it may express itself except through the community leadership which the men who are its officers provide in its behalf.

This is possible only because the time when the emphasis was solely upon the legal entity as such has passed. No longer does that terrifying phrase *ultra vires* stand as a bulwark for cupidity and prevent boards of directors from doing the things which, as human beings, they know they ought to do.

It is now everywhere recognized that the survival of the corporation and the survival of the nation are inseparable; that the welfare of the community from which the corporation draws its profits is a matter of immediate and daily concern to the stockholders.

The man of broad education senses this and, without for a moment slackening his effort for the production of goods and services at a profit for his institution, does all that he can for the social advancement of the society about him.

His opportunities for thus expressing the good citizenship of his company are infinite, as varying and appealing as the needs of the community itself. He takes a hand in education, in the administering of the social agencies of his community, in the development of sound political thinking and good government, in recreation and the care of youth, and in all of the other varying manifestations of modern social life.

He knows that free enterprise itself is on test everywhere, even in our own country, and that the proponents both of socialism and communism offer to the underprivileged the prospect that their welfare will be better served under their way of life than under ours. In fact, the corporation is a symbol of their attack on the capitalists' way of life, and they employ our concept of the legal entity as the symbol of selfishness, rather than as the symbol of service.

In addition, the new challenge of liberal education, as it finds expression through the lives of those who serve corporate enterprises, is to lift the eyes of the businessman so that he may see the world as an integrated whole, and not merely limit his sights to our national borders.

Patriotism is one of the oldest virtues, but love of our own country need not imply hatred of others. Intense nationalism, which in recent years has had such an important development in many nations, is the antithesis of true patriotism, and the task of education is to bring more men to see this.

Few American citizens today have endeavored in their own minds to think through the question of just what should be the end purpose of American policy with respect to other nations, yet the welfare of our children and grandchildren may well depend upon how well we answer that question.

Two great wars have been fought in my lifetime. I believed that both were fought for the preservation of democracy. If that be true, then it would seem desirable to try to advance the cause of democracy by the methods of peace.

Yet will we accept the same burden for the advancement of our ideals in peacetime that we courageously assume in time of war? Military sacrifice we accept with pride and resignation, but the same causes seem to lose their glamor when the bands stop playing.

Surely our own democratic way of life will be more secure for the generations to follow if we are surrounded by countries that likewise practice democracy, than if the world is dominated by despots; but the sense of urgency leaves us when the knife is not at our throats.

Following the last war, the American people accepted the great burden of the Marshall Plan, solely on the basis that their military security was thus advanced. In dealing with the problems of reconstruction of Europe, we neither sought gratitude nor received it at times. We conferred benefits on other nations not for their good but solely for our own, in order that with stronger allies we might feel safer.

But as the military tension eases, for which we all devoutly pray, the world changes, and new challenges appear.

The threat of the Soviets, for example, in dealing with the developing countries is a new and special challenge to a business community based upon free enterprise. Through the destruction of freedom, the Russian ruling caste has created for itself a power which no free nation delegates to its governing group, and which no nation which seeks to preserve private initiative and free markets can match. Nothing like this new threat has ever been seen in history. If this power is ruthlessly employed in the world of international commerce, it can have a profound impact on the economic future of our country.

I know of no specialized form of education which a young businessman might presently take which could equip him for the meeting of such new challenges, but I am sure that the solution lies outside the field of technical training. Such problems, and there will be many more, must be attacked by men of resilient intellects whose educational disciplines have equipped them boldly to attack abstract questions for which they have had no special training.

The eyes of the teeming multitudes in the backward parts of the world are watching us and our way of life, and one further thought is in their minds. They say that what we have achieved is magnificent, but that the process has been slow in comparison with that of our competitors, the Russians. They say that Russia has achieved in thirty years what it has taken us 175 years to accomplish, and that perhaps it would be wise for them to take the short cut. Not having been reared amid our standards of freedom, they are not too sensitive to limitations on liberty. They look the other way at talk of what might happen if they should take Russia's path toward economic strength.

The thing that they do understand, however, and that they do take exception to about our way of life is our alleged insensitivity to spiritual and cultural values. They accept our technology and are happy to imitate it. They also accept our superficial manners, such as lipstick and jazz. But they are not sure that we have a higher culture that is worth imitating. They hold the strong conviction that the emphasis in our way of life finds expression only in material terms, and they do not want their new societies erected on that foundation.

Here is the greatest challenge of all for the men with liberal education.

The truly educated man who lives worthily at no time permits material considerations to dominate his life. When serving a corporation, he never forgets that there are values which transcend tons of production and dollar volume of sales. He knows that the end of life is not the production of goods as such, but an effort to make it possible for more human beings to pursue the good life, as they conceive the good life to be.

This is the lesson that we must teach the world.

The young man who entered American industry at the time when the physical conquest of our continent was under way, when the railroads were spanning the prairies, the steel mills were being built and the great banks were being established, must have had great excitement from the prospects that lay ahead of him.

Today the challenges are far greater, far more exciting. Young men with vision will see this, and will accept the new responsibilities with eagerness and without fear.

The rewards for living worthily transcend anything that human history has known. They will go to those who, by cultivation of the mind and illumination of the spirit, reach the highest level of inner growth.

For Further Information

Listed below are the names of persons connected with educational organizations and institutions who can provide complete information on programs of liberal education they now have available for executives:

Mr. L. L. Smith, Director
Institute for Civic Education
University of Akron
Akron 4, Ohio

Mr. Jerome Ziegler
The Executive Seminar
American Foundation for Continuing Education
19 South La Salle Street
Chicago, Illinois

Walter B. Rideout, Director
Program for Bell System Executives*
Northwestern University
1813 Hinman Avenue
Evanston, Illinois

Mr. Robert W. Craig
Aspen Institute for Humanistic Studies
Aspen, Colorado

Mr. Robert F. Richards, Director
Liberal Education for Business Leadership
University of Denver
Civic Center Campus
Denver 2, Colorado

* Open only to members of the Bell System.

Professor W. Rex Crawford, Director
Institute of Humanistic Studies for Executives
University of Pennsylvania
Blanchard Hall
3446 Walnut Street
Philadelphia, Pennsylvania

Dr. Floyd A. Bond, Director
Business Executives Program in Liberal Arts
Pomona College
Claremont, California

Mr. Granville D. Davis, Executive Director
Institute for Executive Leadership
Memphis Adult Education Center
Southwestern at Memphis
2000 North Parkway
Memphis 12, Tennessee

Mr. Bennett E. Kline, Director
Personal Development Program
Wabash College
Crawfordsville, Indiana

Book Lists

Below are listed the current reading lists for a number of the programs of liberal education for executives. The reader should bear in mind that these programs are of varying length and intensity; the lists alone do not give a full picture of the programs themselves. In almost every case the program includes a number of activities in addition to reading. For addresses, see "For Further Information." However, these lists will suggest something of the flavor and substance of the various programs.

The University of Akron
Institute for Civic Education

A Liberal Education Program for Business and Industry

FRANCIS R. ALLEN *et al., Technology and Social Change*
RUTH BENEDICT, *Patterns of Culture*
DANIEL, "Useful Objects Today"
CARTER HARMON, *A Popular History of Music*
HERZBERG *et al.,* "Job Attitudes"
PARK, "The Philosophy of Education"
STEPHEN C. PEPPER, *Principles of Art Appreciation*
JOSEPH S. ROUCEK, *Social Control*
A. Q. SARTAIN *et al., Psychology: Understanding Human Behavior*
HENRY W. SPIEGEL, *Current Economic Problems*
FRANCIS HENRY TAYLOR, *Fifty Centuries of Art*
MORTON WHITE (ed.), *The Age of Analysis: Twentieth Century Philosophers*
WILLIAM H. WHYTE, JR., *The Organization Man*
"The Contemporary Challenge to American Education," Educational Policies Commission pamphlet
The Executive, Harvard University, Baker Library, Graduate School of Business Administration (March–August, 1959)
The Nation, August 17, 1957
3 "Vital Issues" papers on education

The American Foundation for Continuing Education
The Executive Seminar

Major Readings:

EDWARD BELLAMY, *Looking Backward*
SOPHOCLES, *Antigone*
GEORGE BERNARD SHAW, *Saint Joan*
ALBERT CAMUS, *The Fall*
ARTHUR MILLER, *Death of a Salesman*
HERMAN MELVILLE, *Billy Budd*
T. S. ELIOT, *Murder in the Cathedral*
ALAN PATON, *Too Late the Phalarope*
PLUTARCH, *Lives:* "Cato"
LEO TOLSTOI, *The Death of Ivan Ilych*
EUGENE O'NEILL, *The Iceman Cometh*
FËDOR DOSTOEVSKY, *The Brothers Karamazov:* "The Grand Inquisitor"
LORD CHARNWOOD, *Abraham Lincoln*

Selected Readings for Discussion:

1. WORK

SIGMUND FREUD, *Civilization and Its Discontents*
C. WRIGHT MILLS, *White Collar: American Middle Classes*
DANIEL BELL, *Work and Its Discontents*
RICHARD S. W. EMRICH, "Man at Work in God's World"
BENJAMIN F. FAIRLESS, "Man at Work in God's World"
POPE LEO XIII, "Catholic Social Principles"
POPE PIUS XII, "Catholic Social Principles"

2. THE EXECUTIVE

ALFRED NORTH WHITEHEAD, *Adventures of Ideas*
WILLIAM H. WHYTE, JR., *The Organization Man*
RALPH WALDO EMERSON, "Literary Ethics"
LINCOLN STEFFENS, *The Autobiography of Lincoln Steffens*
NICCOLÒ MACHIAVELLI, *The Prince*

3. THE PURPOSES OF BUSINESS

PETER F. DRUCKER, *The Practice of Management*
R. L. BRUCKBERGER, *Image of America*

4. STATE AND CORPORATION

CHARLES A. BEARD, *The Myth of Rugged American Individualism*
PETER F. DRUCKER, *The Concept of the Corporation*

JAMES BURNHAM, *Containment or Liberation?*

NIKITA S. KHRUSHCHEV, *The Crimes of the Stalin Era: Special Report to the Twentieth Congress of the Communist Party of the Soviet Union*

DEAN ACHESON, *Power and Diplomacy*

13. EDUCATION

ARISTOTLE, *Politics*

BERTRAND RUSSELL, *Why Men Fight*

ROBERT REDFIELD, "The Educational Experience"

14. RESPONSIBILITIES OF BUSINESS

PETER F. DRUCKER, *The Practice of Management*

THEODORE LEVITT, "The Dangers of Social Responsibility"

THEODORE V. HAUSER, *Big Business and Human Values*

THORSTEIN VEBLEN, *The Theory of the Leisure Class*

15. DECISION-MAKING

CHESTER I. BARNARD, *The Functions of the Executive*

FRANCIS BACON, *Novum Organum*

ABRAHAM LINCOLN, Letter to Horace Greeley

THUCYDIDES, *History of the Peloponnesian War:* "The Melian Conference"

MOHANDAS K. GANDHI, *Non-Violence in Peace and War*

DEAN ACHESON, "Thoughts About Thought in High Places"

Northwestern University
Program for Bell System Executives
(Partial List)

Course: *Art in the Modern World*

JAMES MARSTON FITCH, *American Building: The Forces That Shape It*

SIGFRIED GIEDION, *Space, Time and Architecture: The Growth of a New Tradition*

E. H. GOMBRICH, *The Story of Art*

WILLIAM M. IVINS, JR., *How Prints Look*

Course: *Business Decisions and Social Goals*

ADOLPH A. BERLE, JR., *Economic Power and the Free Society*

KENNETH E. BOULDING, *Principles of Economic Policy*

ROBERT L. HEILBRONER, *The Worldly Philosophers: The Lives, Times, and Ideas of the Great Economic Thinkers*

CALVIN B. HOOVER, *The Economy, Liberty and the State*

Course: *Literature as Art and Expression*

ROBERT GORHAM DAVIS (ed.), *Ten Modern Masters: An Anthology of the Short Story*

THEODORE DREISER, *An American Tragedy*

WILLIAM SHAKESPEARE, *Antony and Cleopatra*

JAMES K. ROBINSON and WALTER B. RIDEOUT (eds.), *A College Book of Modern Verse*

Course: *Man in Society*

STUART CHASE, *The Proper Study of Mankind: An Inquiry into the Science of Human Relations*

A. B. HOLLINGSHEAD, *Elmtown's Youth: The Impact of Social Classes on Adolescents*

ROBERT K. MERTON, *Social Theory and Social Structure*

WILLIAM H. WHYTE, JR., *The Organization Man*

Aspen Institute for Humanistic Studies

FIRST WEEK

First Day

THE PUTNEY DEBATES: "An Agreement of the People"

THOMAS HOBBES, *The Leviathan* (Selections)

JOHN WISE, *A Vindication of the Government of New England Churches*

Second Day

JOHN LOCKE, *Treatise on Civil Government* (Chapters 1, 2, 3, 4, 5, 7)

SAMUEL JOHNSON, "Taxation No Tyranny"

The Declaration of Independence

THOMAS JEFFERSON, "On the Constitution"

Third Day

HORACE MANN, "The Importance of Universal Free Public Education"

CORRESPONDENCE OF ADAMS AND JEFFERSON: "On Aristocracy"

ALFRED NORTH WHITEHEAD, *The Aims of Education*

Fourth Day

> ARISTOTLE, *Politics* (Book I)
> PLATO, *The Republic* (Book VII)

Fifth Day

> WILLIAM GRAHAM SUMNER, *The Challenge of Facts*
> ANDREW CARNEGIE, *The Gospel of Wealth*
> LINCOLN STEFFENS, *The Autobiography of Lincoln Steffens:* "Big Business"

Sixth Day

> HENRY DEMAREST LLOYD, *Wealth Against Commonwealth*
> THEODORE ROOSEVELT, *New Nationalism*
> WOODROW WILSON, *The New Freedom*

SECOND WEEK

Seventh Day

> PLATO, *Apology, Crito*
> NICCOLÒ MACHIAVELLI, *The Prince*
> *Alien and Sedition Acts,* 1798

Eighth Day

> ALEXIS DE TOCQUEVILLE, *Democracy in America*

Ninth Day

> *Preamble of the Mechanics Union,* 1827
> *People vs. Fisher*
> *Relations Between Labor and Capital:* Testimony of Samuel Gompers *et al.*
> WILLIAM M. LEISERSON, "For a New Labor Law—A Basic Analysis"

Tenth Day

> KARL MARX and FRIEDRICH ENGELS, *The Communist Manifesto*
> NORMAN THOMAS, "The Future: Socialism?"
> HENRY C. SIMONS, "A Political Credo"

Eleventh Day

    HERBERT HOOVER, "Rugged Individualism"
    FRANKLIN D. ROOSEVELT, Commonwealth Club Address
    ROBERT A. TAFT, "The Republican Party"
    HARRY S. TRUMAN, "The Fair Deal"

Twelfth Day

    WALTER LIPPMANN, *U. S. Foreign Policy: Shield of the Republic*
    FRANKLIN D. ROOSEVELT, "The Four Freedoms"
    WENDELL WILLKIE, *One World*
    Charter of the United Nations
    MARTIN WIGHT, *Power Politics*
    JAMES BURNHAM, *The Struggle for the World*
    ROBERT M. HUTCHINS, "On World Government"

University of Denver
Liberal Education for Business Leadership

PLATO, *Apology, Crito, Republic, Ion*
MAJOR WALTER E. WEESE, "An Introduction to General Semantics," United States Air Force Academy
MARK TWAIN, *The Adventures of Huckleberry Finn*
ALFRED NORTH WHITEHEAD, *Science and the Modern World*
JOHN DEWEY, *Theory of Valuation*
HOMER, *Iliad*
SOPHOCLES, *Antigone, Oedipus Rex*
BREWSTER GHISELIN (ed.), *The Creative Process: A Symposium*
OSCAR WILLIAMS (ed.), *The Pocket Book of Modern Verse*
DANTE, *The Divine Comedy:* "The Inferno"
V. GORDON CHILDE, *Man Makes Himself*
MAURICE R. GROSSER, *The Painter's Eye*
ARNOLD J. TOYNBEE, *Civilization on Trial, The World and the West*
WILLIAM SHAKESPEARE, *The Merchant of Venice, King Lear*
ALEXIS DE TOCQUEVILLE, *Democracy in America*
ROBERT L. RICHARDS, *Dictionary of American Literature*
FREDERICK JACKSON TURNER, *The Frontier in American History*

HENRY JAMES, *The American, The Ambassadors*
ALDOUS HUXLEY, *Brave New World*
JOSEPH CONRAD, *Heart of Darkness*
ARTHUR MILLER, *Death of a Salesman*
JOHN DOS PASSOS, *Manhattan Transfer*
F. SCOTT FITZGERALD, *The Great Gatsby*
ERNEST HEMINGWAY, *The Old Man and the Sea*

University of Pennsylvania
Institute of Humanistic Studies for Executives

General

L. W. WYLIE, *Village in the Vaucluse*

Logic

MONROE C. BEARDSLEY, *Thinking Straight*

Music

AARON COPLAND, *What to Listen For in Music*
PAUL HENRY LANG, *Music in Western Civilization*

World Art

DAVID M. ROBB, *The Harper History of Painting*
DAVID M. ROBB and J. J. GARRISON, *Art in the Western World*
FREEDMAN *et al.*, *Looking at Modern Painting*

Economic History and Thought

WILL DURANT, *The Story of Civilization*
ROBERT L. HEILBRONER, *The Worldly Philosophers*
T. S. ASHTON, *The Industrial Revolution*
ARNOLD J. TOYNBEE, *A Study of History*—2 vols., abridgment
WERNER JAEGER, *Paideia: Ideals of Greek Culture*
CRANE BRINTON (ed.), *The Portable Age of Reason Reader*

Literature

HOMER, *Odyssey*
SOPHOCLES, *The Theban Plays*
VIRGIL, *The Aeneid*
DANTE, *The Divine Comedy: "The Inferno"*
MIGUEL DE CERVANTES, *Don Quixote*
WILLIAM SHAKESPEARE, *Hamlet*
JEAN MOLIÈRE, *The Misanthrope*

GOETHE, *Faust*

PIERRE CORNEILLE, *The Cid, Cinna*

JEAN RACINE, *Andromache, Athaliah, Britannicus, Phaedra*

Literature: Part II

THOMAS MANN, *The Magic Mountain*

FËDOR DOSTOEVSKY, *Crime and Punishment*

GUSTAVE FLAUBERT, *Madame Bovary*

HERMAN MELVILLE, *Moby Dick*

LEO TOLSTOI, *War and Peace*

JAMES JOYCE, *Ulysses*

RICHARD M. KAIN, *Fabulous Voyager: James Joyce's Ulysses*

ANDRÉ MALRAUX, *Man's Fate*

ALBERT CAMUS, *The Plague*

EUGENE O'NEILL, *Long Day's Journey into Night*

WILLIAM Y. TINDALL, *Reader's Guide to James Joyce*

TENNESSEE WILLIAMS, *A Streetcar Named Desire*

THORNTON WILDER, *The Matchmaker, Our Town, The Skin of Our Teeth*

ELIZABETH DREW, *Discovering Poetry*

OSCAR WILLIAMS (ed.), *The Pocket Book of Modern Verse*

T. S. ELIOT, *The Complete Poems and Plays*

ARTHUR MILLER, *Collected Plays*

Social Science

ROBIN M. WILLIAMS, *American Society*

ROBERT K. MERTON *et al.*, *Sociology Today*

DON CALHOUN *et al.*, *Introduction to Social Science*

SOLOMON E. ASCH, *Social Psychology*

Ethics

E. I. MELDEN, *Ethical Theories*

B. F. SKINNER, *Walden Two*

LEO TOLSTOI, *The Death of Ivan Ilych, Hadji Murad*

ALBERT CAMUS, *The Fall, The Stranger*

ARCHIBALD MacLEISH, *J.B.*

C. S. LEWIS, *The Abolition of Man*

PLATO, *Apology, Crito, Euthyphro, Protagoras*

SIGMUND FREUD, *The Future of an Illusion, A General Introduction to Psychoanalysis*

WILLIAM JAMES, *The Will to Believe, Human Immortality*

GEORGE GAYLORD SIMPSON, *The Meaning of Evolution*

DOUGLAS V. STEERE, *Work and Contemplation*

W. KAUFMANN, *From Shakespeare to Existentialism*

REINHOLD NIEBUHR, *An Interpretation of Christian Ethics*
RUTH BENEDICT, *Patterns of Culture*
ERICH FROMM, *Man for Himself*
ALDOUS HUXLEY, *Brave New World*
ROLLO MAY et al., *Existence*

History and Meaning

Scientific American (eds.), *The Universe, The New Astronomy, Lives in Science, New Chemistry, Automatic Control, Plant Life, The Planet Earth, The Physics and Chemistry of Life, Twentieth Century Bestiary, Atomic Power*

American Civilization

MAX LERNER, *America as a Civilization*
RICHARD B. MORRIS, *The Basic Ideas of Alexander Hamilton*
SAUL K. PADOVER (ed.), *Thomas Jefferson on Democracy*
GEORGE R. TAYLOR, *The Turner Thesis Concerning the Role of the Frontier in American History*
COLSTON E. WARNE, *The Pullman Boycott of 1894*
BENJAMIN M. ZIEGLER, *Immigration: An American Dilemma*
C. VANN WOODWARD, *The Strange Career of Jim Crow*
JAMES B. CONANT, *The American High School Today*
Life Magazine, *The Crisis in American Education*
FUND FOR THE REPUBLIC, *Religion and the Schools*
HERBERT AGAR, *The Price of Power: America Since 1945*
DAVID RIESMAN, *The Lonely Crowd*
WILLIAM H. WHYTE, JR., *The Organization Man*
JULIA DAVIS, *The Shenandoah*

Political Science and International Relations

ROCKEFELLER BROTHERS FUND, *International Security: The Military Aspect; The Challenge to America: Its Economic and Social Aspects; International Economics; The Pursuit of Excellence*
Atlantic Monthly Perspectives
COUNCIL ON FOREIGN AFFAIRS et al., (eds.), *The United States in World Affairs, 1947–1958*

City Planning

G. BREESE and D. E. WHITEMAN (eds.), *An Approach to Urban Planning*

Pomona College
Business Executives Program in Liberal Arts

JOSEPH CONRAD, *Heart of Darkness*
OSCAR WILLIAMS (ed.), *The New Pocket Anthology of American Verse*
ROBERT PENN WARREN and ALBERT ERSKINE (eds.), *Short Story Masterpieces*
WILLIAM H. WHYTE, JR., *The Organization Man*
ROBERT L. HEILBRONER, *The Worldly Philosophers: The Lives, Times, and Ideas of the Great Economic Thinkers*
DOUGLAS BUSH (ed.), *The Portable Milton*
WILLIAM SHAKESPEARE, *Hamlet*
FRANCIS BACON, *Essays, Advancement of Learning, New Atlantis and Other Pieces*
SUSANNE K. LANGER, *Philosophy in a New Key*
ERNST CASSIRER, *An Essay on Man*
KENNETH BOULDING, *Principles of Economic Policy*
GEORGE ORWELL, *Animal Farm, 1984*
ALFRED NORTH WHITEHEAD, *Science and the Modern World*
RUTH BENEDICT, *Patterns of Culture*

Southwestern at Memphis
Institute for Executive Leadership

Unit One

COLUMBIA ASSOCIATES IN PHILOSOPHY, *Introduction to Reflective Thinking*
RICHARD HOFSTADTER, *Great Issues in American Politics*
PLATO, *Apology, Republic*
ALFRED NORTH WHITEHEAD, *Science and the Modern World*

Unit Two

The Book of Amos
JOSEPH CONRAD, *Heart of Darkness*
T. S. ELIOT, Selected Poems
FREEDMAN *et al.*, *Looking at Modern Painting*
ROBERT FROST, Selected Poems
NATHANIEL HAWTHORNE, *The Scarlet Letter*
LEWIS MUMFORD, *Art and Technics*
GEORGE ORWELL, *1984*

ALAN PATON, *Cry, the Beloved Country*
PLUTARCH, *Lives:* "Lycurgus"
E. LLEWELLYN QUEENER, *Introduction to Social Psychology*
EDWARD ARLINGTON ROBINSON, Selected Poems
ALBERT SCHWEITZER, *Out of My Life and Thought*
WILLIAM SHAKESPEARE, *Hamlet*
SOPHOCLES, *Antigone, Oedipus Rex*
P. A. SOROKIN, *Crisis of Our Age*

Unit Three

HENRY ADAMS, *Democracy, The Education of Henry Adams*
MARQUIS W. CHILDS and DOUGLASS CATER, *Ethics in a Business Society*
RALPH WALDO EMERSON, Selected Essays
The Federalist, Selected Papers
LOUIS M. HACKER, *The Shaping of the American Tradition*
FRANCIS PARKMAN, *The Oregon Trail*
MARSHALL A. ROBINSON et al., *An Introduction to Economic Reasoning*
ADAM SMITH, *The Wealth of Nations*
R. H. TAWNEY, *Religion and the Rise of Capitalism*
WILLIAM H. WHYTE, JR., *The Organization Man*

Wabash College
Personal Development Program

ANGUS ARMITAGE, *World of Copernicus*
HARRISON BROWN, *The Challenge of Man's Future*
RITCHIE CALDER, *The Science in Our Lives*
HENRY STEELE COMMAGER, *America in Perspective: The United States Through Foreign Eyes*
MILTON CRANE (ed.), *Fifty Great Short Stories*
THEODOSIUS DOBZHANSKI, *The Biological Basis of Human Freedom*
T. S. ELIOT, *The Wasteland*
CHARLES ELTON, *The Ecology of Animals*
The Federalist
F. SCOTT FITZGERALD, *The Great Gatsby*
SIGMUND FREUD, *The Origins of Psychoanalysis*
GEORGE GAMOW, *The Birth and Death of the Sun; One, Two, Three . . . Infinity*
ERIC F. GOLDMAN, *Rendezvous with Destiny*

NATHANIEL HAWTHORNE, *The Scarlet Letter*
ERNEST HEMINGWAY, *The Sun Also Rises*
DAVID HUME, *Enquiry Concerning Human Understanding*
ALDOUS HUXLEY, *Brave New World*
WILLIAM JAMES, *The Varieties of Religious Experience*
H. D. F. KITTO, *The Greeks*
ARTHUR KOESTLER, *Darkness at Noon*
WALTER LIPPMANN, *The Public Philosophy*
SAMUEL LUBELL, *The Future of American Politics*
NICCOLÒ MACHIAVELLI, *The Prince*
JOHN STUART MILL, *On Liberty*
ARTHUR MILLER, *Death of a Salesman*
PLATO, *Apology, Crito, Republic*
EDWARD SAPIR, *Language*
JEAN PAUL SARTRE, *The Flies*
Scientific American (eds.), *The Physics and Chemistry of Life*
WILLIAM SHAKESPEARE, *Hamlet, Macbeth*
GEORGE BERNARD SHAW, *Saint Joan*
ADAM SMITH, *The Wealth of Nations*
SOPHOCLES, *Antigone*
JOHN STEINBECK, *The Grapes of Wrath*
JOHN H. STORER, *The Web of Life*
JONATHAN SWIFT, *Gulliver's Travels*
HENRY DAVID THOREAU, *Walden*
ALEXIS DE TOCQUEVILLE, *Democracy in America*
LEO TOLSTOI, *War and Peace*
MARK TWAIN, *The Adventures of Huckleberry Finn*
THORSTEIN VEBLEN, *The Theory of the Leisure Class*
VOLTAIRE, *Candide*
WALT WHITMAN, Leaves of Grass
OSCAR WILLIAMS (ed.), *Immortal Poems of the English Language*

The Writers:

GILBERT W. CHAPMAN is President, The Yale and Towne Manufacturing Company.

FRANCIS H. HORN was President, Pratt Institute, Brooklyn, New York

E. DIGBY BALTZELL teaches sociology at the University of Pennsylvania.

WILFRED D. GILLEN is President, The Bell Telephone Company of Pennsylvania.

MORRIS S. VITELES is Professor of Psychology at the University of Pennsylvania.

RUSSELL KIRK is author of *The Conservative Mind* and other books, and editor of *Modern Age*.

FRANK W. ABRAMS, citizen at large, was formerly Chairman of the Board, Standard Oil, New Jersey.

RALPH BARTON PERRY (1876–1957) was Professor of Philosophy at Harvard University.

ALFRED NORTH WHITEHEAD (1861–1947), one of the most distinguished philosophers of his time, was in his latter years at Harvard University.

FREDERIC E. PAMP, JR., is with the American Management Association as a Division Manager.

JAMES C. ZEDER is Vice-President, Chrysler Corporation.

PETER F. DRUCKER is Professor of Management, Graduate School of Business, New York University.

JOHN CIARDI is Poetry Editor, *The Saturday Review,* and Professor of English, Rutgers University.

FREDERIC R. GAMBLE is President, American Association of Advertising Agencies.

A. M. SULLIVAN is Editor, *Dun's Review and Modern Industry;* author of several books of poetry.

MORTIMER J. ADLER is founder-director, The Institute of Philosophical Research, San Francisco, California, and has lectured recently in liberal studies for Industrial Indemnity Company and Inland Steel Company.

J. ROBY KIDD is Director, Canadian Association for Adult Education.

RORERT J. BLAKELY is Vice-President, The Fund for Adult Education.

H. W. PRENTIS, JR., is Chairman of the Board, Armstrong Cork Company.

CHARLES A. NELSON (*see below*)

CLARENCE B. RANDALL was Chairman of the Board, Inland Steel Company.

The Editors:

ROBERT A. GOLDWIN is Director of Research, The American Foundation for Continuing Education, Chicago.

CHARLES A. NELSON is head of his own management consulting firm, Nelson Associates, White Plains, New York.